Crazy
or
Not,
Here I Come

RYAN D. BURD

Fulton Books, Inc.
Meadville, PA

Published by Fulton Books 2020

ISBN 978-1-64654-878-1 (paperback)
ISBN 978-1-64654-879-8 (digital)

Printed in the United States of America

Special thanks and love to…

Pamela E. Hatten, my mother, who brought me into this world and never stopped caring for me and taught me what the true meaning of family and unconditional love is.

PREFACE

This writing I've done is about a very ordinary guy who's gone through a very extraordinary experience. The events that transpired during this journey inspired me to share the experience. The need to write this book became more and more obvious as time went by. This book is written from the perspective of a man experiencing something but not knowing what that experience is and the journey that follows.

This topic was forced upon me almost ten years ago but has forever changed my life in ways that are truly remarkable. This experience may have happened to you, but you just never knew what you went through, or you may be going through it right now. Either way, this book is intended to let you know you're not losing your mind, you're not going crazy, and you're not alone. Trust in yourself and enjoy the ride!

CHAPTER 1

Happy New Year, I Think

A crazy thing happened to me on my walk through life. I woke up. Well…wait a minute. Maybe I should say I began to wake up. People in the know call it an "awakening." It didn't matter that I didn't know what the hell that was at the time because it was about to happen to me, and like it or not, I would never—and I mean never—be the same again. I guess there's a lot of different ways that this happens to people. The funny thing is, there's no way to see it coming and no way to prepare for it. It's not like other events that you can put on your calendar and plan for. It doesn't work like that. I'll tell you how it worked for me, and if I could be totally honest, I would have preferred a different way, but nothing ever came easy for me in this life. Why should this be any different?

It's a very painful process in many ways, and it turns out you don't get to pick the time, and you sure as hell don't have anything to say about the place either. I'm not sure who or what chooses the time and place for it. I often wonder, was it what we call "God"? Or was it my higher self? Or maybe before I incarnated here, I chose the time and place. I haven't figured that out yet. I'm still going through this crazy episode in my life. I've just started experiencing my awakening, but any of these possibilities are mind-blowing if you ask me, but I digress. We'll chat about this more later on.

Mine began with a complete breakdown I had on the first of January 2011, and it almost cost me my life. To say things hadn't been going well for me for some time would be a damn understatement. To be completely honest, my whole adult life hadn't been going well for me, and it had pretty much been a screwed-up mess for as long as I can remember. I'm sure you know people like that in your life. They just can't get their shit together no matter what they do. Somehow, I muddled through it though; but in the last couple of years before my breakdown, I really twisted my life up.

I'd been looking for work for almost two years, and I couldn't find anything. I mean it was unreal. I couldn't find a damn job to save my life, and ironically, that's exactly why I was looking for one—not to just save my life but my families too. I'd never had this problem before, and trust me if there was one thing in this world I was good at, maybe the only thing I was ever good at, it was finding jobs. I've had over forty-five jobs in at least thirteen different fields and industries. That's a shitload of jobs, and those are just the ones I can remember, and it doesn't account for any of the temp jobs I had along the way either.

I need to tell you there's something I feel you need to know before I get any further into the strange story I call my life. I hope it will help to put my situation into proper perspective because I was screwed. I didn't have any money, I couldn't borrow any money, and I had no credit either. I can't even find the words to tell you how dire my situation was.

I don't consider myself to be a stupid person by any stretch of the imagination, and I don't think anyone that knows me would say I was either. I never had a lot of money even though I had a degree in electronics and was certified to be a travel agent and also certified and had a class-A license to drive tracker/trailers as well. I was the epitome of a paycheck-to-paycheck kind of guy. For Christ's sake, I never made more than twenty-nine thousand dollars in a year, and I was forty-four on the day my egg cracked. I mean the day I had my breakdown. Just think about what I just said for a minute. Not more than twenty-nine thousand dollars in a year. That's nothing in today's world. Is it sinking in yet? I mean I was underachieving bigtime in every sense of the word. I was what people called a loser. They might not call me that to my face, but they definitely thought it. That went for family, friends, and anybody that knew me for that matter.

That alone was enough to put a person into a depressed state. Never mind the overall emotional state I was in at the present time, having to deal with all the other bullshit going on in my life. The desperation of my situation was wearing on me. It was grinding me down day after day, week after week, month after month, and year after year until I was just a shadow of who and what I used to be or wanted to be.

I'd been unemployed and out of unemployment benefits and food stamps for some time. I also had a few businesses that failed during that time period, which put me even further into the

CRAZY OR NOT, HERE I COME

hole financially. Just to make ends meet while I looked for work, I spent all my family's savings, maxed out all our credit cards, and cashed in all our investments we had, which wasn't much; but you do what you got to do when the shit is hitting the proverbially fan, and trust me, it was. It was hitting the fan in buckets.

I had to go to churches wherever I could find them to wait in line for the boxes of free food they were passing out to the poor and homeless in the area. I guess I was one of them too now. I got really good at going online and finding the churches. They were always in the worst part of the Atlanta metro area. Sometimes I had to drive quit a distance to churches to get those boxes. There were times I would wait in line with people you never would've thought would be there, but there they were. These people were from all walks of life. It was scary and very humbling because life can turn on you in a heartbeat.

I can tell you there's plenty of time to think about your life and all the mistakes you've made and the situation you're in because of those mistakes when you're waiting to get your box of food. It was at those times I think I felt the worst. I thought it couldn't get any worse and how that could even be possible, but I was so wrong. I was wrong about so many things back then, and now I had to file bankruptcy too. Oh yeah, that's right, and that was the icing on the cake. That was the last straw. It was the final nail in the coffin as they say. I didn't know what I was going to do now, but what I did know was, with a bankruptcy on my record, I was out of options now. I couldn't borrow money anymore, I had no credit cards anymore, and I couldn't find a job either. At this point in time, I can tell you it really sucked to be me. I was drinking more than ever now. If I was awake, then I was drunk or working on it. I was beginning to spiral out of control, and I couldn't stop. I was getting more and more depressed. I did what I could to hide my pain from my wife and family, but it was hard. I told myself everything was okay, but I knew that wasn't true.

Well, you ask. What do you do when you're already at rock bottom and as low as you can go on the ladder of life? Let me think. Oh, I know. I guess there's only one thing left to do. I may as well have a complete fucking breakdown, and that's exactly what I did in grand fashion.

That fateful day started out pretty good. It was January first and the start of a brand-new year. I remember thinking, *I can't go through this crap another year*, and telling myself this was going to be the year I get myself together. I got up and started drinking mimosas with my wife. My daughter was playing in the family room. I went up to my man room and was watching the college pregame shows, and my wife stayed downstairs in the kitchen, talking on the phone and working on making a big new-year's break-fast. She was taking her time, and that was fine with me because that gave me time to polish off quite a few mimosas. When those were gone, I started hitting the hard stuff. I don't know exactly how many whiskeys and cokes I had, but this was where things got a little sketchy for me. This was where it all started. I would never be the same again; I just didn't know it at the time. How the hell could I?

What happened was, all the intense stress that I had been dealing with for the last two and half years, especially the humiliation that I felt coupled with a lifetime of compartmental-ized stress that I'd been carrying around with me because of all the screwups and failures in my life, finally surfaced, or should I say erupted. I think the booze triggered something deep inside me. It somehow opened or released or shut down or bypassed the mechanisms I had in place to keep my stress suppressed and under control, but the genie was out of the bottle, and there was no way that sun of a gun was going back in. You see, it was showtime. I was the lead performer, and the show was about to begin.

I blacked out at some point before my wife had finished making breakfast. I say "blacked out" because I don't know how else to describe what happened to me. I mean it was like I was awake but trapped inside myself. I guess I was conscious on some level, but not completely aware of what I was doing. I don't remember everything except bits and pieces of what happened or what I did during that time, which was about two to three hours.

What I'm going to tell you now are things I can recall and things told to me by my wife and my mom as best as they can remember. It's funny, though; they couldn't remember as much as they thought they'd be able to. I think they needed to block out those memories. I think on some level that day was more traumatic for them than me.

It was weird. I came downstairs, ranting and raving about nothing and everything at the same time. Tears were running down my face. I could hear myself, but I didn't know what I was saying. I was raging. I was in an uncontrollable, agitated, and very confused state of mind. Something had woken up inside me, and I'd never been like that before or since that day.

My wife and daughter were sitting at the dining-room table, just talking and eating breakfast, when I came down stairs. I was crying and yelling and saying all kinds of crazy stuff. This went on for a while. It scared my daughter so bad she hid under the dining-room table. Till this very day I struggle with guilt for the horror I inflected on her that day. I guess my wife tried to calm me down, but to no avail. By now she was afraid, no, terrified—terrified for my daughter and afraid for herself—and she should have been because I was completely out of my mind. She could see it in my eyes. At this moment her loving husband of eighteen years, the husband she knew, was gone, and what she was dealing with now was something she didn't understand. At some point, I think she tried reaching my older brother, but it was my mom that got a hold of him first and told him what was happening. He lived about twenty miles from my house in Georgia. As I continued to rant and rave about God knows what, my wife was able to rush my daughter out to the car and lock the car doors in case I followed them, and she hauled ass for my brother's house. My wife and daughter were gone, and I have no memory of them leaving. Till this day I still can't remember them leaving. I do, however, remember going up to my "dad room" and getting my handgun and grabbing the bottle of whiskey from the kitchen.

Then I blacked out again for a while. At some point, I guess I called my mom because when I came to, or zoned back in, I was on the phone with her. I could hear myself talking. No, I was raging, but again I couldn't understand what I was saying. It was like someone else inside me was speaking through me. I must have scared the crap out of my poor mom. She knew this was the real deal. She felt it. Her worst fears of her son's situation were about it happen. She could hear the pain and rage in my voice. She knew I was beyond depressed, alone, drinking and carrying a loaded handgun, and she was 3,300 miles away in Oregon on the other end of a phone. Her mind was racing, and yet sometime during the call, she had the presence of mind to have my stepfather call the police in the city where I lived in at that time. She must have used my stepdad's phone to call my brother and told him to get over to my house right now! My brother could hear the fear in my mom's voice, and he knew something was horribly wrong.

She kept me on the phone, which wasn't hard to do. I was still raging, crying, and rambling incoherently. The police arrived at my home minutes later. When I heard a knock at my door, it was my mom that told me to answer it. She knew it was the police. I answered the door. I'd set my handgun on the couch while I was on the phone with my mom, and it had slid down in between the cushions. It wasn't visible from the front entranceway at my house where the police officer was standing. My mom hung up when she heard the officer's voice, knowing she could do no more, and prayed for the best.

The officer began asking me questions. I walked over grabbed the bottle of whiskey off the coffee table and sat down on the couch right next to my handgun. The officer took a few steps in but stayed in the entranceway and also kept the front door opened about halfway. He continued to talk at me, but I was gone. I was in the darkest depths of my mind.

Somehow, with my mind in complete chaos, a thought had popped into my head. It was a devilishly evil thought and the perfect way to end it. You know, to kill myself. To be totally honest, I'd be lying if I said I hadn't thought about killing myself many times in the last couple of years. I figured my wife could remarry to someone who could provide for her much better than I ever could, and my daughter was young enough that she wouldn't have much memory of me or this day as she got older. In time she'd have a new dad to care for her and give her the things she needed that I never could give her. This was my thought process. I was so withdrawn and in a place so dark I actually thought that killing myself was not just an option but the best option. It made perfect sense at the time. I wouldn't have to feel this pain anymore. I couldn't live one more day with it, and my family would be able to move on without me screwing everything up in their lives.

So what was my devilishly evil thought? As I sat there on the couch right next to my handgun that was wedged in between the cushions and perfectly hidden from the officer, I thought I could just draw on the officer, and he wouldn't have any choice but to pull his sidearm and defend himself and fire on me. I wouldn't have to technically kill myself, but I'd be dead just the same, the pain all gone and all my problems solved. As a bonus, my wife and daughter wouldn't have to tell people that I killed myself. I could go out with a little dignity, which was the best possible way out, given my situation.

Now this was where I believe divine intervention came in. I've thought about this moment in my life over and over and over. It's the only answer I have at this point and time. The officer was still talking because I could see his lips moving, but I didn't understand a damn thing coming out of his mouth. I gripped my handgun tight, so tight my hand hurt. I put my finger on the trigger. I remember starting to sweat a lot, and I took another big chug off the whiskey bottle that was in my other hand. My mind went blank. I was ready to do what I knew had to be done to end all this bullshit, to end all the pain. After all, this was best for everybody involved; and in my screwed-up state of mind, I really believed it was. What's really crazy is, after forty-four years of life and everything I've been through, it all came down to this. The end of the road for me was nothing more than a goddamn bottle of whiskey in one hand and a loaded handgun in the other. No more thinking; it was time, so I began to pull my handgun from the couch cushions.

It was at that very moment my brother walked in. He must have started over to my house right after my wife or mom called him earlier. When I saw him walk in, I pushed my handgun back in between the cushions. When he looked at me, I saw in his eyes how scared he was. It must have hit him the minute he saw me that the situation was so much worse than he had imagined. As I looked at him, he stared back at me for what seemed like an eternity; and then I stood up, and I walked over to him, and we embraced as only brothers could, and he told me, "I need you, bro. I love you, man," and at that instant everything I felt inside—all the rage and the anger and the confusion—just subsided. It truly is amazing how those words defused the situation. It wasn't that all my problems were over, and I didn't know how or what I was going to do now, but I was alive, and my heart wasn't beating a mile a minute anymore. I wasn't at peace, but I was calm now and much more coherent. That moment changed my life forever and was truly the beginning. We talked to the officer for a few more minutes, and he left, feeling the situation was over. It was for him, but for me, my journey had just begun.

CHAPTER 2

What Just Happened?

When I woke up the next morning and I saw my wife sleeping in our bed, I had only one thought pop into my head. I got up and went to my daughter's room. I had to see her. I had to know she was okay. I guess my wife and daughter came home later that evening after I had passed out.

It was strange, though. When I saw my daughter, I had this incredibly intense wave of energy that tingled and rushed through my body. It was like someone gave me a shot of adrenaline. It started in my legs and rushed quickly up to my head. When it reached my head, my eyes began to well up and water. It was as if some of that energy had to be released because it was too overwhelming for me to handle. Tears streamed down my face. I was overcome with emotion. I've always been an emotional person, but this was different. I remember thinking, *I love my kid, but goddamn, this is crazy.* That was the first time I felt something—I mean something that I couldn't explain, something that was just different on every level because it wasn't just human emotion I was feeling. It was bigger and more intense than that.

The following weeks my wife and I never really talked about my "episode," as she called it. I think both of us just wanted to put it behind us and move on. When I looked into my wife's eyes, I could tell she never wanted to talk about it... ever! My daughter was young, so Mommy just told her "Daddy was upset about some grownup stuff," and she didn't need to be scared anymore because Daddy was okay. It seemed like it was "case closed."

Then one night about, a month later, I was up in my "don't fuck with me now" room. Just kidding. I mean up in my dad room. I just like calling it that sometimes. I was watching some TV, and I recall looking at the clock, and it was 11:14 p.m. I remember the time. I don't know why I just do. I was lying on my couch, dozing off while the TV was on. I was at that point where I was somewhere in between being conscious and not really being conscious. Its kind a hard to explain, but we've all been there, and it's a strange place to be. It's like half your mind is in this world, and the other half is…well, somewhere else.

Then I heard a voice. I remember it clearly because it was a women's voice, and it sounded familiar to me somehow. It said in a very loud whisper, "*Ryan!*" It was like someone was standing right next to my couch when they said it. It startled me, and the hairs on the back of my neck stood up. It scared me because I thought someone was in my house. I popped up off the couch and turned in the direction it came from, but there was no one there, nothing, just a dark hallway, that's all. I thought, *What the hell is going on?* Not long after hearing that voice, at least I think it wasn't long after hearing that voice, I found myself standing there, looking around my room, and this was where everything got weird. I was really kind of freaking out.

It was bazaar because my whole room looked like I was seeing it through water, or maybe like I was surrounded by water. I don't know exactly how to explain it. It was kind a like looking at a coin you might see at the bottom of a shallow riverbed. Its size was all distorted, and it looked like it was moving, but it wasn't. That's exactly what was happening in my room. Everything in my room—the walls, the floor, and even the window—looked like they were moving or rippling or waving back and forth and in and out, but with a certain ebb and flow to it all.

I don't know if I was awake or dreaming. I think somewhere in between is more like it. While I was in this state of being or state of mind or state of consciousness or state of whatever it was, I had this tremendous sense of "presence" wash over me. It was overwhelming to say the least. I had this incredibly fantastic, warm feeling resonating within me as it engulfed me and took my breath away ever so gently. It was so beyond awesome and so damn beautifully terrifying at the same time. It was immediately followed by a totally awesome sense of "knowing" that came over me. It just filled me up. I'd never felt anything like it before or since. The feeling was angelic! There were no words spoken, but I knew in my very being and all that I was that this "presence" was nothing to be afraid of and nothing to fear. It surrounded me and penetrated me down to the core of what I was. It knew me in every way possible. It knew what I was, what I am, and what I'll ever be. It's like it imprinted "truth" right into my mind, like someone taking a syringe and injecting me with it. I know how crazy this all sounds. If it hadn't happened to me, I don't know if I'd believe it. I've got to tell you, this whole experience is incredibly hard to describe. How do you describe or explain something that you've got no context for? I really think there truly is no way to put into words what happened to me. I'm simply doing the best I can with the limited amount of consciousness I possess. It just felt so far beyond me.

Time seemed irrelevant during the whole experience that night in my room. When I became aware again, I looked at my clock, and it was just after four a.m. Just less than five hours had passed, but to me, it felt like only a few seconds had gone by. How can that be? In my mind, as quickly as the experience started, it was over; but in the real world, almost five hours had passed.

I just laid there on my couch, dazed and confused for some time, staring out my window till the sun came up, trying to understand what I just experienced. I couldn't, but I had this incredibly ominous feeling that something was coming for me or looking for me or that something was out there waiting for me to find it, just wanting to be found, but what, I didn't know.

What I did understand after that night was, there is what I call a "divine presence." I don't like the term "God" because it just doesn't seem to do justice to what I experienced. I know it exists because I felt it and experienced it. It doesn't matter what anyone else believes or doesn't believe or what anyone thinks about what I'm saying. It makes no difference to me because it's real. I didn't know at the time how it happened or why it happened, only that it did happen. I know that the "presence" I felt isn't just out "there" somewhere, but it's within all of us. It's everywhere. We're connected to it somehow, I think by our consciousness. I lost my faith that night, and it was the most wonderful thing to ever happen to me because I no longer just have to believe "God" exists. I know it exists. That "presence" is the most awesome feeling I've ever felt.

I could write an entire book on what happened to me that night in my room. I could go in a hundred different directions, speculating on what it was I felt and experienced that night in my room, but why? In the end, all the speculation and all the "what-ifs" would be just that speculation and "what-ifs." Maybe I'll never understand it. Maybe there is no understanding it. Maybe it's just beyond our concept of understanding or knowing. Maybe just knowing it exists is all we ever need to know about it. Only time will tell.

I'm cool with that because for me, it's enough to just know that it happened; and in time, maybe I'll truly understand the magnitude of what it was that I experienced that night. At that time in my life, I was just meant to know that the "divine presence" is real, and it exists. It's like I was given just a little taste of its awesome power and its truth.

When I think back on that night, I always get that rush, the same one I got when I went into my daughter's room after my breakdown, and I tear up. After all the crap I've gone through in my life and all the crap I'm still going through, that experience gives me strength now. It's because there had to be a reason for it. To me, it feels like I was chosen. I might be wrong, but that's how it feels to me. Things like that don't just happen to everybody that much I know, and I know on a very deep level that it means something, but what? There are two questions that linger in my mind since that experience I had that night that bother me because I don't have the answers to them. Why me, and why at that time?

If you're reading this and want me to tell you it was "God," I can't. Maybe it was, maybe it wasn't. I just think that our whole concept of what we call "God" is completely wrong. I do know it was beyond name and beyond form, I can tell you that. It was beyond comprehension, but at the same time it wasn't. If what you're reading bothers you or makes you feel uneasy, maybe it's because there's a part of you that isn't so sure what you've been told by your religion is true. Keep reading, and maybe you'll find the answer to that question, or just throw this damn book away and go back to reading the stuff that fits into your comfort zone, or should I say your "lifebox."

Even as I write these words all these years later, I still find myself questioning what happened, but I think that's normal for what I'm going through. It's no coincidence, however, that right after that strange experience in my room, the process of my awakening truly began. Almost overnight literally things I never gave any thought to I began to question, and the harder it became to deal with normal everyday stuff, things 99 percent of the population don't give a second thought to. I found myself questioning and resisting, and I didn't understand why. Not yet anyway. I didn't understand why other people couldn't see what I see or feel what I feel. Till this day it still frustrates me and drives me crazy!

My experience left me with two obvious questions: Why me? And why now? All these whys, why this and why that, it drove me crazy. I couldn't get these whys out of my damn head, and trust me, I didn't need any more crap up there. There was enough already. I slept for what seemed like days after that night. I was pretty much completely mentally and, yes, physically drained at this point.

I didn't know what my breakdown had started. I was clueless about what was happening to me, and in some respects, that night in my room didn't help either. That's why I truly believed I was going off the deep end. I didn't find out about what the hell was happening to me until sometime later down the road on my journey.

I spent the next couple of weeks trying to get back to somewhat of a normal life, or least what had become normal for me. I did the best I could to get myself into a routine, looking for work, finding churches giving out the food boxes, and doing everyday "dad" stuff. I always just told myself it'll be okay when I knew deep down, I was so full of it. I was scared and alone, and there wasn't anyone I could talk to either. I definitely wasn't going to tell my wife about my experience that night. She already was worried to death about me. I just had a complete breakdown and almost killed myself, and now I'm going to tell my family that I was hearing voices too. I don't think so. Even I'm not that crazy! I think?

The days and weeks that followed, I still couldn't shake the feeling that something was coming or waiting for me out there. It was an unsettling feeling. I think it was kind a like when an animal knows a storm's coming and feels anxious. I was so conditioned by all the disappointments in my life I just knew this feeling I had of something coming or waiting for me had to mean something bad was on the horizon. That's how broken inside I was. That's how empty I was inside. I was so disconnected from myself. I'd been living my life, if you can call it that, consciously and spiritually asleep. I didn't know I was conditioned and controlled by the "ego" when all this started. That kind of concept was completely foreign to me back then. After all, I was Ryan, and I was in control of my life. Everybody has an ego, but don't tell me it controls my life. That's just bullshit, and everybody knows it. That's a bunch of hippie, new-age talk. People who don't want to take responsibility for their actions in life use that kind of crap as an excuse. Don't they?

I just knew I was being tested by God. What else could possibly be going on? I obviously wasn't going to church enough or praying enough or reading the good book enough, and now I'm being punished by God because of it. I still thought and believed I was human, and so I was flawed and needed to be led to salvation. I couldn't have been more wrong about that and everything else, but you see, that's what I learned in my "lifebox." So much has changed since that fateful night in my room. It totally blows my mind when I think about it, and I do, a lot!

I'm changing somehow, but all that change comes with a heavy price. I feel so very isolated and cut off from people, especially the ones I love. I realize now that's just how it works. I know so much more, and my awareness has grown so much. I see things so differently, and I know things that the average person doesn't know or understand. Be careful now. I didn't just say I'm smarter than everybody else who hasn't experienced what I have. That's just what your ego wants you to hear.

I can only tell you my thoughts based on my own experience and hope there'll be people out there who'll resonate with what I have to say about my thoughts and experiences. I don't think anyone will ever confuse me for a writer. I'm not a writer. I'm just writing. That's a completely different mindset, and that's how it feels to me. I don't think I have a writing style, but maybe not having one is my style. Time will tell; it always does. I'm no different from anyone reading this book right now. I'm just some ordinary guy who had some extraordinary things happen to him while living an average life, just trying to get by; but if it can happen to me, then it can happen to anybody!

If you're still reading this, then you've been drawn to my story somehow and someway. It doesn't matter how or why you ended up with this book. All that matters is that you have it now. It's resonating with something deep inside you whether you're aware of it or not. That's how it works. That's all I know. That by itself is a comforting thought. Sometimes just knowing you're not alone has to be enough. That's helped me to just get me to the next day in my awakening. I hope if you're reading this, you truly understand that you're not alone because I'm out here. I often wonder if the real reason why I'm writing this book is to just feel some sort of connection with somebody, anybody, because I've been feeling so cut off from everything and everybody since this whole thing began. I hope it isn't like this for the rest of my life because I need that connection with other individuals that are experiencing this reality in the same way I am. They must be out there…somewhere, I hope.

I've been mentally beaten up and broken into more pieces than I care to think about. I've been bruised and contused and mentally assaulted for my entire life. I've endured more mental anguish than I thought possible, but here I am. There are pieces of me lying all over, from Oregon to Georgia and back to Arizona. I've been putting the pieces of myself back together for years now. So I started doing something years ago after all this crazy stuff started, something to keep me in touch with myself. Every damn morning, when I get up, I hit the bathroom, I stand in front of the mirror, and I look into myself. Not at myself but into myself, sometimes for just a minute and other times for god knows how long, and this is what comes out as I stare into myself: "I'm right here right now." I just keep saying it over and over and over till I'm saying it with purpose and attitude until it sounds like someone else is saying it through me, until I merge with my higher self. There are times I get myself totally jacked while I'm doing this, and that's the point because I'll never give up or give in to whatever it is that doesn't what me to become all that I am. Never!

CHAPTER 3

What the Hell Is Going On?

Fifteen months and a handful of crappy temporary jobs had gone by since my breakdown and the experience up in my room, but I finally found a job. It wasn't a dream job by any stretch of the imagination, but a pretty damn solid one. Well, thank the maker! Don't get me wrong; I was very grateful for the job, and as you know by now, I was that close to breaking! As the saying goes, "Beggars can't be choosy," and I was definitely not going to be. I was delivering propane now for a well-known propane company in Georgia, but the job came with some major drawbacks and a heavy price to pay.

First off, the job terminal I worked out of was located seventy-five miles from my home. I had to drive on all three major highways in the Atlanta metro area to get to and from work. I worked fourteen-hour shifts from five a.m. till seven p.m. I had to leave for work by three thirty every morning. I was scheduled to work to get there by five a.m. It took me an hour and a half in the mornings to get there, but to get home at night, it took me two and a half to three hours because of the brutal traffic in the Atlanta metro area. So every day that I worked turned out to be around an eighteen-hour day. Those were the longest days of my life because I was so tired from my fourteen-hour shift that I worked, and I still had about a three-hour drive to get home when I got off work. Those were tough times, and trust me, it really sucked!

Second, the pure physicality of the job was brutal as well. It was insane. I only worked every other day on Tuesdays, Thursdays, and Saturdays which on the surface doesn't sound like a major drawback, but that was because the job was so damn physical they wouldn't let you work back-to-back days unless it was absolutely necessary.

The third and final drawback and the most problematic was my age. I was going on forty-five, and I already had a lot of rough miles on this body I was in. Let me tell you, propane tanks are heavy. If you're carrying just one of them, they're not bad, but I was carrying about five hundred of them each day I worked or fifteen hundred a week. That's a lot of propane tanks for anybody, let alone a guy my age. They're thirty-two pounds each. I did this job for three years, and it damn near killed me. I would carry about seventy-five thousand pounds of propane a week. How did I know that, you ask? At the end of each day, I got a printout, and it told me the amount of propane delivered, and it was in pounds, not by the number of containers delivered. Till this day I still have problems with my shoulders, my knees, my back, my feet, and my neck. I have no idea how I did it for three years. Well, maybe that's not entirely true, but more on that later.

I was busy again and just so happy to finally be working I hadn't thought about anything for a little while. Nothing really out of the ordinary had happened. I thought everything was behind me, and I was just getting on with my life, but I was wrong again. By now it was April, and things were about to begin to get stranger. I know what you're thinking: it can't get much stranger than what I wrote about in the previous two chapters, and you might be right. That was some pretty wild stuff if I do say so myself.

It's funny in a strange kind of way because the only real memories of those months following my breakdown and my room experience were the feelings of being detached from everybody and everything. That lingers on even till this day. It was like I was on an island by myself with no one else around, and that's how I'd been feeling for some time at that time. I didn't really talk to people very much during that period of time in my life except for family, of course, but even that was difficult. What is going on?

It just seemed to feel like a barrier or a veil was between me and everybody else in the world. I could see them, but they couldn't see me. I felt invisible both physically and emotionally, and that's just how it was for me at that time. I didn't feel like my normal self. I felt somehow different inside, but that wasn't so bad because my "normal self" was pretty messed up most of the time anyway. There was a part of me that had this feeling that something was letting me marinade in the memories of those two events, giving me time to really take it all in. Like I needed time to give myself the chance to accept what happened to me. I knew that was important somehow.

At this point and time, I was confused more than I normally was about things and still was struggling to just get some stability in my life. I'm talking primarily about my mental stability because I couldn't think straight, I was feeling stressed, and in an awfully strange kind of a funk. I didn't know where these feelings and emotions were coming from because they felt different. I should've felt frustrated, angry, and very pissed off at my present situation I was in, but I didn't. Those were dark times for me, and that's saying something because I've experienced some pretty dark times in my life.

It was during my time at the propane company that I started having all kinds of crazy stuff happen to me, things I'd never experienced before. I was receiving or getting what some call "downloads." I didn't know where these were coming from. It was information about all kinds of stuff just slamming through my mind. It was fragmented thoughts, phrases, ideas, snapshots of past times in my life, memories of stuff I'd completely forgotten about and stuff I didn't want to remember. There was so much I couldn't retain all of it, and much of it I wouldn't understand until later on. It made it hard to concentrate on whatever I was doing.

All I was thinking about were the downloads I was receiving. I couldn't get them out of my head. Believe me, I tried, but they were always there. Intuitively, I knew that they meant something. These downloads were trying to tell me something or trying to lead me in a certain direction to something, but I didn't know what at the time. I guess I was a slow learner because it took me a while to begin figuring out and decoding some of them and understanding why I was getting them.

I think about it now, and it doesn't frustrate me; it just really pisses me off. It shouldn't, but it does. I was just so ignorant about what was happening to me. I literally didn't have a clue about what I was going through. It's funny too because I always considered myself to be a spiritual person, but I was beginning to realize just even how wrong I was about that. My whole concept of spirituality was wrong because what my religion had taught me was completely wrong. I began to understand that religion has nothing to do with spirituality. Looking back, I would've thought I'd picked up on what was going on with me from the start, but no, that's not how things were working in my life at that time. I was just such a damn mess inside.

About the same time, I was beginning to receive all those weird downloads in my head,

I noticed that I was seeing things differently. I mean seeing things from a completely different point of view I didn't even know was possible. You know, not just looking at things a little differently but from way out in left field. Things I never gave a second thought about my entire life and things I never really thought about at all were now thoughts rushing through my mind. These thoughts ranged from stuff, like if the universe is really like what we've been told it is, the concept of time, all sorts of questions about the moon and the sun, and the concept of reality to things I saw every day—like the sky, trees, grass, flowers, sunrises, sunsets, birds, butterflies, and even my own cats and dogs—were taking on a whole new level of emotion and realization for me. All of sudden it seemed like everything became so wondrous to me. I could see a beauty in everything, and I'm not exaggerating either; I mean everything!

I also felt so damn connected to everything it was freaky. I could feel what my own pets were feeling now, and yes, I know how crazy that sounds. I could sit in the grass in my own backyard, running my fingers through it and have an angelic experience. Don't get me wrong; it was a wonderful feeling, but I would laugh at myself, thinking, *Jesus Christ, I'm turning into a freaking hippie. All I need now are some flowers and beads in my hair. Somebody, please pinch me and wake me up. What the hell is going on?*

To say my emotions were heightened would be an understatement. I mean my emotions were like off-the-charts kind of heightened. I would have these incredible emotional highs and then go into these incredible emotional lows. These emotional swings could happen anytime anywhere, and they did. It was happening so much after a while it almost became normal to me. I said "it almost became normal." I didn't like it, so I tried not to pay attention to it anymore, but that was impossible. It wasn't something that I could ignore, that's for sure. I just kept lying to myself because that's what I was good at and telling myself, "Everything's going to be all right. You've gotten through so much crap in your life you sure as hell can get through this." Funny thing is, even as I said these words to myself, sometimes in my head and other times out loud, I really never believed it.

I was also beginning to have a hell of a time sleeping. That was something that I guess I took for granted, but I guess most of us do. I mean, you go to bed, and you go to sleep, but not anymore for me. My sleeping habits were thrown totally into chaos. I'd come home after working a long eighteen-hour day, and I used to eat and hit the couch and fall asleep right away like anybody would after a day like that, just like a baby with a full belly, but now I was finding myself gaming and watching stuff on YouTube for hours because I wasn't tired; and when I did finally fall asleep, it wouldn't be for very long. I wasn't sleeping more than a couple of hours at a time, and that's continued till this day.

It's very rare that I sleep longer than four or five hours now. I'll crash out at ten or eleven at night and get up around three in the morning almost like clockwork. I'd wake up three or four times during that period. I never slept more than a couple hours at a time. On a sidenote, waking up at three a.m. is something strange all on its own. I came to understand what that was all about later on in my journey.

On my days off, I'd find myself being completely drained and lethargic during the main part of the day and then feeling more energetic and awake as the evening came. That was totally out of character for me. I was never a night owl. I was always an early bird. So for this to be happening wasn't normal at all! It was really making it hard to do my job because I wasn't getting enough sleep. I needed all the sleep I could get before I began my long days, but instead I struggled to make it through my shifts at work, and then I'd get home, fall asleep for a while, but then I'd wake up and be up all night. It was a brutal cycle that had no end. It was wearing me down both physically and mentally.

About every two weeks on a weekend, I wouldn't do anything except eat and sleep. I was just so exhausted I couldn't do anything else, and it's not like I didn't have things to do on the weekends either. I had yard work to do, and I had a big freaking yard too. I had my daughter's softball games to go to, and I was missing them as well. It was starting to affect my marriage because my wife was getting really pissed off that I wasn't getting stuff done around the house and that I was missing my daughter's softball tournament games as well.

I was really frustrated, and I tried; God knows I tried to explain things to her, but what the hell was I thinking? All she saw was me sleeping all the time. I don't blame her, and I knew my wife wasn't the kind of person to understand the kind a thing I was going through anyway. Hell, I didn't understand it myself. My body was completely out of whack. I guess the best way to describe it is it felt like my body and my mind weren't in sync with each other. My whole world was spinning and changing, and I was just trying to catch up and also keep my family from knowing what the hell was going on with me, but it wasn't easy.

When I did get some sleep, I would dream. I was dreaming a lot, and my dreams were so vivid. They were so lucid, more like memories. I could feel the emotions in my dreams too, and they were intense. I mean very intense! I knew intuitively they were trying to tell me something. I remember feeling so frustrated with myself because I couldn't figure them out. Hell, I still have dreams today that I can't figure out, and I feel just as frustrated. At the time, to be honest, most of my dreams I didn't understand. Only a small percentage of them I did. I really don't know why. I keep hoping one day I'd be able to understand more of my dreams because I just have so many of them.

This awakening forces me to be patient with myself, and that's something that goes totally against my nature. You can't rush through an awakening. It has its own timetable it goes by. I literally dream every night when I go to sleep! I think maybe I need to expand my consciousness more before I'll ever understand a lot of my dreams. It's just that I want to know and understand everything right now, and it just doesn't work that way. This whole process isn't going or moving fast enough for me. I'm slowly learning to just go with the flow.

I understand that just because I'm experiencing what I'm experiencing doesn't mean I know everything and have it all figured out. It's actually quite the opposite; I'm not any smarter than I was before all this. I can't spell any better than I did before or do calculus, mathematical problems now. What's happening is, my consciousness is expanding, which means my awareness is expanding, which means my perception is growing as well. I've gained a much larger outlook of this experience we call life, and yet I still have days of pure confusion. I guess what I'm trying to say is, I'm going through this crazy experience, and it's like a roller-coaster ride; and like all roller-coaster rides, you can't get off until the ride's over. That's how it works, and once this particular ride starts, you can bet your sweet ass you're in for the ride of your life!

Between my job being as physically challenging as it was, all the downloads I was receiving, the amount of dreams I was having at night, my lack of sleep and the emotional roller coaster I was experiencing, I was exhausted. I was really just kind of spaced out. I did everything I could to ignore what was going on with me even though something told me not to ignore it but to embrace it. It's just that there were times during my awakening that I so desperately needed to shut it down and give my mind a rest, and there was also a part of me that was still scared to death of what was happening to me. I was simply too scared sometimes, and because of that, I was spending so much energy trying to ignore everything even though it wasn't working. At all! I found out that I couldn't ignore this awakening experience I was having, and it wouldn't just go away. I wanted to understand my reality and have it make sense to me because that way, I'd feel comfortable. I needed to feel safe in the life I was living. We all need to feel safe in the lives we live.

To make matters worse at the time, I had no idea what an "indigo child or adult" was, let alone what a star seed was or a star child was either. I had no idea what an "old soul" was. I had no idea what an "empath" was. I had no real concept of what an "ego" truly was. I had no real concept of my "conscious self." I didn't understand or know anything about a "higher mind' or a "lower mind," and I sure as hell had no real concept of a "higher self" either. I would soon come to learn of these things, but when I think back on it, I didn't know crap about anything! What really bothered me even till this day is, I had no idea whatsoever how truly small the "life-box" I was living in was. I was so spiritually and consciously asleep I actually thought that being awake meant just waking up in the morning. I was such a naive, dumb ass! I look back and just laugh now because I couldn't have been more wrong about everything I thought I knew. I feel like kicking my own butt sometimes for being so ignorant.

If I'd have known any of these things, it certainly would've made life a little easier at the time, and I think that's maybe the biggest under-statement I've ever said. The crazy thing about all this is, if I hadn't had this experience happen to me, I would've never known about any of these terms and concepts I'm talking about, and all of them now are playing a major role in what I'm now becoming.

It's a funny thing, experiencing what I'm experiencing, because it isn't what you think it would be at all. In fact, the more I learned about other people's experiences like mine, I found myself saying, "Man, mine's not like that at all."

Don't get me wrong; there are a lot of things I had in common with the others but a lot less than I thought. I watched people on YouTube, and many of them are so calm, and they speak so eloquently about my type of experience, and I'm just sitting there, thinking to myself, *What the hell went wrong with mine?* Because what I've experienced so far hasn't brought me to a very calm place at all! There are days that I'm so damn depressed and frustrated with the whole experience I want to blow my head off…again! Now I'm obviously exaggerating, but not by a lot. An awakening is not for the faint of heart. I truly believe people that experience an awakening are chosen to do so. By what or by whom, I don't know at this time, but I have my suspicions of what entities are behind "the choosing," as I like to call it. Let me just say right here as a sidenote, and I don't want you to go crazy, but I just used one of my new original terms I came up with during my awakening experience. I just think that's a really cool thing!

My kind of experience doesn't happen to you overnight. The next morning you don't wake up with wings on your back, a halo over your head, and you don't go walking around, singing religious hymns either. It's a process an individual has to go through all by themselves to achieve its rewards. It's a spiritual experience, not a religious experience. That point really has to be understood, and I can't stress it enough that there's a hell of a big difference between religion and spirituality! It's time people understand that because that's a game changer as they say!

It's been a hell of a thing that I've gone through. It's a very terrifying thing to experience to be sure, and it was really brutal for me because I didn't know what the hell I was experiencing for so long; but the crazy thing is that, at the same time, it's the most beautiful and wonderful experience a person can go through. Does that mean I'm crazy? I don't know…maybe.

It'll scare the crap right out of me and fill me with dread one minute, and then a minute later it'll fill me full of such joy I haven't the words to even describe it. I can say this now for sure. I don't know where I'm being led to or taken to. I don't even know what I'll be when this journeys over, and I don't even know who or what is behind all this yet, but I do know I'm no longer on the road to nowhere, and that is a very cool feeling!

CHAPTER 4

Just a Piece of Me

"Lifebox"—now that's a fantastic word. It's a term that I came up with. At least I think I did? I mean, I've never heard anyone use the term. I introduced this new term in the last chapter, but I didn't expand on the concept. The word just kind a manifested itself as I progressed through my experience. I think that's pretty damn cool if you ask me, but why am I telling you this?

You see, the lifebox I was living in, the one I never knew was even there, was about to open up. Sure, it was going to be opening very slowly in my case because a process like this needed to move slowly to give me time to drink it all in. It was going to take some time for me to adapt to how I was beginning to perceive things now. As I stated before, my awareness was expanding, which, in turn, was expanding my perception, which was changing the way I perceive reality. It's almost like I could see dead people now. Nevertheless, it was going to happen, and so it began, but that wasn't the thing that really blew me away. Sure, it was going to be a whole new experience, and my world was going to change, but what really freaked me out was the realization that I even had a "lifebox" in the first place!

I came to understand that we all have a life-box we live in, and my lifebox was my limited view, and I mean very limited view, of this reality I live in as well as my very limited view of myself. I worked and slaved on my lifebox without rest— day in, day out, week in, week out, month after month and year after year until I created the pre-fect barrier. I created the perfect lifebox. I lived in it in pure ignorance and went through life with a total lack of understanding about everything going on around me, but the most humiliating and frustrating thing for me was the fact that I was so damn ignorant about what was going on inside me. I didn't know or understand myself at all. I truly had no idea of whom or what I was, and I certainly had no idea as to why I was even here. It's hard to believe I lived, if you want to call it that, for forty-four years like this, but all that was beginning to change. This ride I was on was off and running, and there's no way of getting off, but maybe deep down I don't really want to.

A little more time had passed, and I was starting to calm down a bit and think a little clearer. Understanding some of the information or downloads that were slammed through my mind wasn't really happening yet, or I should say it was happening but slower than I wanted it to. I was curiously being drawn to stuff I never had any interest in ever before. I would end up doing things that I didn't have any conscious memory of thinking about wanting to do. Why all of a sudden was I having all these thoughts about these things? I didn't know at the time why, but that's what was happening to me.

One night I was on my gaming system, and I was looking at some of the apps that were available. I'd never done that before. I'm a little old-school, and I just used the system to play games. I've brought only two things I like to do with me through life from childhood: one was my love of video games and the other my love for playing the drums.

Now I've been playing video games since the game, Pong, came out way back in '77. I was eleven years old at the time, and it was the best time of my life because I was just a very young soul experiencing this reality the way it was meant to be experienced with joy, wonder, and pure amazement. Anyway, as I was looking at the apps, I came across one, and I'd heard of it before, but I never gave a moment's thought about it. I could've cared less, but for some unknown reason and totally out of character for me, I loaded the app this time and began checking out what it was all about. I don't really remember how long I'd been checking it out when I ran across a video that asked, "Are you an indigo?" and before I knew it, I'd found the first missing piece that would help me begin the process of putting myself back together. It was only one piece, but by the time I was done understanding what it meant, I felt a little more whole and a little less broken up inside for the first time in my life.

Remember when I told you about that rush I got when I went into my daughter's room the morning after my breakdown? Well, when I came across this video on this app about indigos, I got that same rush again. That's how I knew to watch it. Ever since then, I get that rush every time I'm thinking the right thoughts about something, or I'm seeing or hearing something I needed to see or hear, and also every time I'm in a place I need to be in too. I've come to trust that feeling completely.

That rush of energy was the first thing that I intuitively knew was guiding me at the beginning of my experience or my journey; yet I was still fighting it or resisting it to some degree. I think because on a certain level it scared the hell out of me, but I couldn't ignore it, and I couldn't convince myself as hard as I tried that it wasn't real or happening to me. It wasn't a voice or a dream that I could easily dismiss. When I felt that rush, it took my breath away, and it moved me emotionally. There was no denying it, no way at all.

As I watched the video about indigos, I started hearing what one was and learning what the indigo characteristics and personality traits were. I couldn't believe what I was hearing. I had to pause the video for a few moments because I was rushing hard again. Tears were filling my eyes and rolling down my face. It was hard for me to see the screen for a few minutes. My mind was popping like flashes on a camera, and I began seeing a lot of past events that happened in my life. It was a mental overload.

As I was watching, I realized something instantly. It hit me like a damn lightning bolt, and for the first time in my life, I understood why I thought the way I did and acted like I did and did things the way I did them; why I saw the world we live in so differently and felt so different from other people too. It answered so many of the whys I had about myself. I could hardly believe what I was hearing. I sat there on my couch in total amazement that night for hours, watching as much as I could about indigos. I was like a sponge, just soaking it all in. It was like watching someone talk about me, telling me things only I ever knew about myself, and I couldn't get enough. In a way, I felt kind of validated because all the things I did throughout my life I was beginning to understand. I knew without a doubt that I found a piece of me that I was missing.

For me that was a very powerful thing, and it really impacted me tremendously in a very positive way. I had all the characteristics of an indigo, not most of the characteristics but all of them. It was freaky, and to have this new understanding of myself was amazing.

I'd always felt broken up inside, like a part or parts of me were missing. I never felt complete or whole, but now I found a piece of me that was missing, and just like that, literally overnight, I felt a little more balanced and complete. I was slowly beginning to understand what a blessing it was to be experiencing whatever it was I was experiencing. I used to look in the mirror, and I didn't know who or what was looking back at me, but now I knew I was an indigo.

Now when I looked into the mirror, I had some sense of positive identity for the first time in my life. I wasn't just seeing some dumb, fat loser who never achieved anything and didn't have a clue. I could tell myself proudly I was an Indigo! Absolutely goddamn right! I actually felt a little special now and a little more confident too. That's something I'd never felt before, and you know what? It felt really good! It wasn't anything my parents did to me or didn't do for me that made me feel not special, and my parents had no part in me not developing any confidence either. It was years of self-abuse and years of listening to that record player in my head play all my favorite negative thoughts over and over and over. I didn't even need other people to put negative thoughts in my head anymore because I was doing it well enough all on my own. I was such a mess sometimes when I think about it, I just want to scream!

I wanted so badly to tell everybody, or anybody for that matter; but it was my secret, and no one would know it. No one could know it. It's a strange thing. On one hand, I wanted to tell whoever would listen what I discovered about myself; and on the other hand, I knew it wasn't the kind of thing that anybody I knew would understand. Everybody would just think I'm flipping crazy. It's like, how do you explain to a blind man what the color red looks like? It's sort of flipping impossible. I also knew whoever I told wouldn't understand how much it meant to me personally, but with all that aside, it was still truly one of the best days of my life.

As time passed, I was slowly realizing I'm not as crazy as I thought; and in the back of my mind, I couldn't help but wonder what led me to find this out in the first place. I mean, I'd lived forty-four years without knowing I was an indigo. Why now? I knew somehow it had something to do with the breakdown I had and all the weirdness that followed, but I didn't know what or how it was connected. I knew for sure that something was happening to me because I could feel it. That had become perfectly obvious. I might have walked, talked, looked, and sounded the same on the outside, but I sure as hell wasn't the same on the inside. I realized after my experience that night in my room that change was heading my way, but so much of what I was experiencing just felt so unreal. I was confused, I guess, and didn't really know what to think.

Did I lose my mind that fateful day? Hell, I didn't know. Then weeks later I had that strange experience in my room, and then those energy rushes, the downloads, the lucid dreams, my problems sleeping, the heightened sense of emotions, the feeling of being connected, and now I find out after all these years that I'm an indigo. All these things can't just be coincidences. I feel like I'm going farther and farther down the proverbial rabbit hole.

I knew it was time to embrace what was going on with me and to trust it and, even more importantly, to find out what it was that was happening to me, but I was still scared. I knew I needed to find the courage somehow to do it. I'll just have to give it time, but after around four months of craziness that was going on, I finally saw something good come out of this experience. It was something absolutely amazing, to be more precise. It gave me a boost of confidence, one that I so desperately needed. I think I mentioned it before—it had been a long time since I felt confident about anything. I'd been struggling for so long, especially the last couple of years.

Time seems to pass very quickly for me now. I turn around, and *wham*, another month has passed and another one and another one. I think a good year or so had passed, and during that time, I spent all my free time whenever I could to get some research and learn everything I could about indigos. The more I learned about them, the more I learned about myself as well.

I was spending a lot of time reflecting back on my life, and the one thing that kept popping into my mind was all the jobs I had. I had at least forty-five jobs in at least fourteen different industries that I can remember, and now I knew why I had so many jobs in my life. I wasn't some nut bag, and I wasn't a lot of the things society told me I was. Society was wrong about me. Praise the Lord for that! I wasn't all screwed up after all. I just had no true concept of who or what I was. It wasn't because something was wrong with me, and I wasn't suffering from some flavor-of-the-month mental problem like attention-deficit disorder either. That's just what society told me. That's what the professionals told me, and let's face it, the professionals are never wrong…right?

It was because I was searching for something, but I didn't know what it was. I never could shake that feeling. I've had it my whole adult life. I just didn't realize that what I was searching for was myself. I was just going from job to job, looking for who and what I was, when the whole time I should've been looking within myself. I had no idea just how disconnected I was from myself. I realized that was the first of many of what I now call a "knowingism." They come over me now ever since all this began. They just pop into my mind, and they're not from my conscious mind either. I felt they came from beyond my thoughts, but at the time, I didn't know where those thoughts or ideas came from. I intuitively knew they're very important, meaningful, and most of all, they're truth for me to know and understand. In the beginning, all the "knowingisms" I was given were about me; but as time went on, they were about other things too, things that challenge all we've be taught about this world we live in.

I told you I've always felt broken up inside. What I should've really said is that I felt broken apart, and it felt like pieces of myself were missing. I guess that's all part of this experience that I'm going through, to find one's self; to know and understand the concept of "self" that's something worth contemplating for a while. That's something worth truly knowing and understanding.

I knew I wasn't going to find "me" or my "self" at some damn job I had. I don't care what the job was or what I was doing or what my damn job title was. Until I figured out what I'm here to do, no job will ever be satisfying for me! The problem was that society teaches us that you are what you do, but sorry, that's complete bullshit! We've created this awful beast of a thing we call a "society," and it wants you to think you don't really have an identity until you have a title behind your name. What you are is what you are, and what you do is what you do. Those are two totally and completely different things. Most people are confused by this, but as I said, "those are two completely different concepts." When I write these words, I try not to come across sounding like an angry person even though I am a little angry because I experienced firsthand how that way of thinking or programming messes with people's minds. It sure as hell confused and messed with mine for many years.

I always had these feelings and thoughts that it was the world that was all screwed up, not me. My therapist told me that I was experiencing what they call "denial." I never agreed with that diagnoses. I always thought that was a bunch of bullshit! I couldn't put my finger on it, but I knew something wasn't right. Everything I saw or felt just seemed so superficial to me, but it's easy to doubt yourself when the rest of society is telling you every day that you're the one that's all screwed up.

Then one day I was thinking—no, I was contemplating, which I do a lot more since this whole thing began—and it hit me. I'm seeing that everybody's got a mask on, not one that any person can see but people like me, "indigos," can see. I can see people's masks, and I see the real person who's hiding behind it, and I can feel their energy too. I was always able to do that. I just never paid much attention to it, but now my senses and intuition have gotten much more acute. That's why I was never drawn to your mainstream, popular personality types. You know, the ones everybody likes and wants to be around because I could see behind their masks. I didn't like what I saw, and I didn't like the vibes I got from them either, at least not from most of them anyway.

I could feel their ugliness, and I understood their self-serving ways, but I could also feel their sadness. I could feel the scared little child inside them, the one that they hide from the rest of the world.

I was always drawn to the outcasts or the geeks of the world, those people that society labeled as different or weird, but I found those types to be the most honest, genuine, and kind people I'd meet. I got good vibes from those people because they were real. They felt no need to wear masks. You see, our so-called modern societies can only work if everybody's wearing their masks. Societies would crumble if people started taking their masks off. It's the mask that people wear that allows the system to manipulate the populous. The whole system would have to change if people could truly be themselves. It saddens me profoundly because most people are so afraid to just be themselves. You would think it would be the easiest thing in the world to do, but it' not. It's one of the ways people lose touch with themselves and why they can't see what they really are. It's part of the reason the world has become so sick.

I felt there had to be more to life, specifically my life. That's why I got so bored and uninterested with jobs so quickly. The jobs had no real meaning and no depth of feeling to me. I went from job to job, searching for purpose in my life and an identity too, but I wasn't finding either of them. It's odd. I should've known if I couldn't find my purpose at one of these jobs, I sure as hell wasn't going to find myself either. Damn, how stupid could I be? How didn't I see any of this? I was just so spiritually and consciously asleep, that's why, but I guess I was persistent if nothing else. I like to think that accounts for something anyway. I think maybe that's the only thing that did get me through life up to this point.

You know, I could always tell if someone was being less than truthful to me, and I could always feel when a person was being insincere. It wasn't anything I had to try to do to be able to do it. It always came naturally for me from as long as I can remember. I was always the one to notice when no one else did, but I never thought that it meant I was special. I actually used to hide this ability from everybody because I didn't want to feel any more different than I already did.

Why can I do this? Why can't anybody else see and feel what I can? Where does this ability come from, and who or what gave it to me? I could never understand that, but it turns out, it's a very strong indigo trait. On the surface, you'd think it was a good thing, and it is in many ways, but it also caused me a lot grieve. It certainly didn't help me make new friends because I didn't do well with having casual conversations with people. I just went through the motions during conversations like that because I really had no interest in them. I like to call it "pillow talk"— you know, really generic and safe topics; the stuff you'd talk about at a party with a girl you're trying to score with or with a coworker at work. I can do it, and I do it more than I want to, but it feels so forced for me.

It just seems so easy for people to waste so much of their time talking about nothing. When I look back, I know this is one of the reasons I didn't have many friends, but I guess I never really wanted or felt the need to have a lot them. It meant more to me to have a few very close friends than to have a lot of them. I understand more now about how and why I interacted with people the way I did during my life. It's a bitter-sweet feeling. I'm happy I know now, but I'm sad I didn't know sooner.

One characteristic I discovered about indi-gos that really resonated with me was, they feel like they're not form here, and I've felt like that my entire life, not because of anything my fam-ily ever did to me. I love my family more than life itself, and I know they love me too. I used to think that whoever brought me here or whatever put me here did so and then forgot about me.

It's a horrible feeling to feel abandoned, but that's how I felt; and I still feel that way today, but now I understand why.

I know intuitively that this physical reality that we live in isn't my home. Funny thing is, I don't know exactly where my real home is or how that works yet, but I do know that I'm not from another planet or galaxy or anything like that. It's more of a knowing, or "knowingism" as I like to say, that I belong naturally in another form and another place far away, yet probably right here. Another dimension, if you will, but it's still confusing. I don't think we've been told the truth about what's called the universe and many other things as well. I know how that sounds, and in time I'll explain what I mean, but that will be in my next book.

Everything has its price, and finding out I was an indigo had one too. Knowing this only intensifies the feeling of isolation and loneliness that I deal with every day, and I know I'll probably have to deal with it for the rest of my life. What's really ironic is, the more people I'm around, the more alone and distant I feel from all of them.

I know I'll always be different. I'll always be the odd one in the room and the black sheep of the family, the guy that does things differently and acts and says things differently than everybody else, but there's another price to be paid that I'm talking about.

Besides feeling alone and distant from people, there's one feeling that bothers me tremendously even today. It's the inability to really connect with people and have them really know and understand me. My heart aches to be understood on a very spiritual and conscious level with real depth of feeling. It leaves me feeling like I'm invisible to the rest of world and especially to the ones I love. When I think about it, and I think about it more than I should, it's just another thing I have to deal with as I learn and understand more about what I am.

As I write these words, I never thought that I'd be struggling the way I'm struggling to just talk about myself and the things I've gone through. Trying to explain what's going on in my mind and in my own little world is a lot harder and scarier than I ever thought it would be. There's a part of me that's so afraid of everybody thinking I'm batshit crazy when they read this book; yet at the same time, there's another part of me that really doesn't care because I am what I am, and I experienced what I experienced. I've never felt so compelled to do anything in my life like I was to write this book. I try not to think about it, but I can't help but wonder sometimes if I'm just to broken to be fixed, but that thought passes, and I just tell myself, "Don't look back, just keep going."

All these things I've been talking about are all characteristics of indigos that I also have, but these were by no means all the characteristics of an indigo. I saw the world and interacted with it the way I did because that's what I am. I'm very proud I'm an indigo, and it's a pretty cool feeling to be one too. It's a gift, but what's difficult for me to deal with sometimes is how differently my life could've been if I'd only known all this stuff and figured it all out decades earlier.

I wouldn't have had to suffer for all these many years and put myself through all the mental anguish I put myself through. I punished myself pretty good my entire life. All that led to me medicated myself with whatever I was into at the time, and that went on for far too long. My life would be forever changed if I'd only known, but then again, I understand I wouldn't be who I am now if that had happened. Everything had to happen the way it did in my life, but there's just no way around it; there's always a price to pay. It sounds corny, and I never thought I'd ever say this and really mean it, but I am really getting to know myself, and I mean truly getting to know myself like most people never do. Let's be real. Most people are too afraid to face themselves. When they look in the mirror, just the body they're in is all they'll ever see. They'll never truly see themselves, and that breaks my heart every time I think about it.

After giving a lot of thought about what I've gone through the last couple of years, I just said, "Screw it. My life is what it is, and if I'd come this far, then I sure as hell can go a little further." I'll get up every damn morning and tell myself today's the first day of the rest of my life, and I'm going to make it count!

CHAPTER 5

Just How Old Am I?

Well, those damn downloads just kept coming! You know what, though? I figured something out while they were slamming through my tiny little mind. It took a while, but hell, this whole process I'm seeing is going to take a while. Evidently, I have a lot to learn and a lot to unlearn as well. I get the feeling that whatever is sending me these downloads knows that, and I'm sure it's pretty obvious to see.

Sometimes I felt like a child who's holding his mother's hand and being led around because he needs that much help and guidance to get to where he needs to be. It was because I was so disconnected from myself and so broken apart inside. I look back on it now, and I realize just how blind I was. I was so lost, of course, I needed a guide to guide me. It felt like I was being given instructions on how to find myself and put myself back together. Sometimes I just wanted it all to end, but I knew that wasn't happening anytime soon.

I would get mass amounts, or what seemed liked mass amounts, of information in a very short time span. It would be overwhelming, and then I started to notice a pattern, and I saw that certain bits of information would replay in my mind more often than others would. This would go on for a while—as long as needed, I guess—and then those bits of information would get more specific in nature.

During a download session, I would get a lot of information; mostly it was thoughts and ideas about whatever it was that was being conveyed to me at that particular time. Pictures and snapshots of things happened less frequently, but they still happened quite often. Time just flew by as I mentioned earlier, and it might have been around two years. I don't really remember exactly how long I'd been knee-deep into all the information about indigos when I started getting bits and pieces of fragmented thoughts in my mind about the subject of life and death.

Little by little, all those fragmented thoughts and images of life and death began to grow and come together and form a more concrete picture in my mind, but those were still pretty broad topics to think about. I would find myself at work, driving and delivering those damn propane tanks, and I would get lost in thought with the downloads I received. I wouldn't even remember accounts I serviced because I'd be so deep in thought with the information I had banging around in my mind. I was so preoccupied with all this crap in my mind I was having trouble concentrating on anything I was doing. It's like my body was in one place, but my mind was somewhere else far away.

I saw myself as just another average guy. There wasn't anything special about me, and yet I had all these really deep thoughts in my mind that wouldn't go away. You know, the kind of thoughts that only philosophers and smart people have, not people like me; not people that are struggling to just get to the next day in their life. Yet there I was, thinking of stuff, like what does it mean to live or be alive? What does it mean to die? How do we know what we call reality really isn't just a dream? When we die, do we realize it? Do we have any memory of living after we die?

When we do die, is that when we really wake up? That's pretty deep stuff for a guy who just delivers propane.

My thoughts were no longer generic in nature. I wasn't thinking about souls in general terms anymore, and I wasn't thinking about life and death and the concept of souls in religious terms either. Like do they go to heaven or hell? My thoughts were turned inward on myself. Why was I living? Was I dreaming all this? What happens to me when I die? What will death mean for me when it's my turn to cross over? I couldn't get any of this stuff out of my head. I was totally consumed with all these thoughts, and I wanted them to stop and just go away, but I couldn't stop thinking about my soul. I had this one thought that really stood out from the others in my mind.

I was thinking about my soul, and what if it wasn't a part of me but just trapped inside this human body? What if I'm the soul, and the body I'm in is just a container for me to be able to interact with this reality? Maybe a soul is just like a driver in a car. It can get in and out of the body like a driver gets in and out of a car, but only at certain times only when the door is able to be opened. I thought death would be the time that the door was able to be opened. I was also wondering, why would I even think of things like that?

I realized that what I was thinking about was the recycling of souls. It was about the reincarnation of souls, but not just any soul—my soul. What is going on inside me? I'm just trying to survive and find a way to take care of my family, and I have all this kind of stuff in my head. It makes no sense, and I definitely didn't have the time to start going crazy again. My wife would kill me if I had another breakdown right now. I've got to pull myself together and get my head straight, but the downloads are getting wilder, and these thoughts in my mind won't stop.

Here I go again! Do souls come back? Are souls just a one-and-done kind of a thing? Are they created just before you're born and then uncreated after you die? I had no idea at the time where these thoughts were coming from. I just knew they sure as hell weren't my thoughts and that they were coming from somewhere or something else.

When things got too intense for me, I would do what I could to shut it down. Usually, that meant drinking until I passed out, but that wasn't working because then I'd start to have dreams about what I didn't want to think about. I quickly understood there was no running from my own thoughts. Whatever was putting this stuff in my head wasn't going to stop and was very persistent.

I would try to lighten my spirits a little when things were getting too serious for me. I would joke that this stuff was a little heavy for a guy who almost killed himself not that long ago. It gave me a little laugh, but that's about all it did. I knew I had to try and keep some sense of humor about all this crap going on, or I wasn't going to make it to wherever it is I was being led to. So that's exactly what I've done over the years. Since I've been on this long, strange trip, I just try to laugh as much as I can about all of it. Laugher really is good medicine.

There was another thought that stuck out in my head more than a lot of the others. It was a thought that really intrigued me, and it was, how old is my soul? Is it timeless and never ending? I found myself pondering this and contemplating this idea for quite a while. I mean, I was never told by any religious leader how that all worked. Did God just think me into existence before I was born, or is there so much more that we don't know, let alone understand? I'm starting to really question what I've been taught by my religion. I'm starting to think they got everything all wrong.

I don't remember reading anything in the Bible about where or what I was before I was born. I don't remember any priest talking about it at church either. All I really heard from my religion in my younger years was what happens to you after you die. If you're a good boy, you go to heaven; and if you're bad boy, you go to hell. Looking back, I know now they got that all wrong too; but at the time, I still wasn't quite sure.

So there I was, two years removed from that dreadful day. I was reflecting on things and wondering about my resent downloads I received about the soul, my soul, other people's souls, and everything else that had to do with that subject. You know, the sort of thing that every delivery driver thinks about. Yeah, right! Then it occurred to me. It hit me like a ton of mayonnaise. I wonder if there are people that actually have insight into this topic but not people who were religiously indoctrinated. Once I had the idea and really gave it some thought, I was like, "You dumb ass, of course, there is. There has to be people out there."

Something was leading me away from the whole religious point of view on the whole soul subject. It was like something was screaming at me to look elsewhere for answers, and it couldn't believe I hadn't thought to do that yet, almost like it had run out of patience with me and said, "Okay, this guy needs some serious intervention." Then something in my head said, "Things got to keep moving, Ryan, because you've got much to know and much to accept for the healing process to begin." I didn't think I could be healed, and I didn't really understand what that meant exactly. I had no idea that the "something" in my head was actually my "higher self" reaching out to me when it could get through my ego's defenses.

So I went to a place I'd become very familiar with as of late and a place that for years to come would help me on my journey in many ways. It was like this app was made just for me. So I fired up my gaming console, logged in to my account, and went on the app. I remember holding the black controller in my hand, and I was trembling with anticipation—anticipation of what I might discover. As I started to type the words "old souls" into the search box, I was instantly filled with that unmistakable rush again. God, it really takes my breath away and fills my eyes with tears every time it happens. I couldn't see the TV screen for a minute again, and I knew, obviously, I was on the right path; but where this path was taking me, I didn't know—as usual.

I hit the enter button, and in seconds my sixty-five-inch TV screen was filled with little boxes. Every box had something to say or do with old souls. I was shocked. I couldn't believe how many there were. My first thought was a comforting thought. I get it a little more often now during my experience, and it always brings a smile to my heart. I thought, *Damn, I'm not crazy!* I've been questioning my sanity during this entire journey, and you will too if it happens to you; but that's okay because you've read my book, and now you know it's completely normal for the most part. You can't go through an experience like I'm going through and not think you're at least a little crazy.

I don't recall how long I sat there clicking on each box so I could read the subject line(s) at the bottom, but it was a while. It was wild because I couldn't decide what box to choose. Then I made the mistake of going back to the search box and typing in something a little different from just the words "old souls," and *bam*, more boxes popped up, and they were different from the first set of boxes I was clicking on. Now I was seriously screwed because I didn't have a clue where to start. At all! I eventually called it a night and went to bed. I felt drained, and my mind was overloaded. I was on such an emotional rush my energy drained very quickly. I hit the pillow, and I was out. I actually slept pretty well that night.

I was up early the next morning. It was Saturday, but my daughter didn't have any softball games that weekend; funny how that worked. So off I went up to my room. I turned on the TV and fired up the game console. Got on the app, did my search, and clicked on the first box on the top left of the screen. The video was about how it's not uncommon that indigos are also old souls as well. I wasn't more than five minutes into it, and I was like, "Here we go again." My body was buzzing from head to toe, and I knew instantly, yep, that's me. I hadn't even heard what any of the old-soul characteristics were, but I knew all the same. I'm an old soul too, no doubt about it. I knew I just found another piece of me, another piece to the "what the hell am I?" puzzle.

My first emotion, though, was one of anger because I felt a little cheated again, and I was pissed. I didn't find out I was an indigo until I was forty-four, and now I find out I'm an old soul when I'm just about forty-seven. Why didn't I know this about myself when I was much younger? In time I would know why, but I didn't then. I was asking that "voice" in my mind, "What's the point of me knowing this truth now?

It's kind of like getting all dressed up and having nowhere to go. What's the point?" I remember being frustrated and thinking how cruel life was. I didn't know if I was angry with God or myself or the world or with whatever led me to this truth about myself. There's just no worse feeling than asking why about something and not getting an answer.

I couldn't stop thinking about being an old soul and what that might mean. I kept taking these tests to see how old my soul really was, but part of me hoped that I would fail them so I'd have an excuse to stop this ride I was on and get the hell off. Maybe I could convince myself that I was just wrong about everything. No, that wasn't going to be happening anytime soon because every test I took told me I was an old soul. It's like the joke's on me, and the universe is having a big laugh on my account.

I was pissed off and frustrated for a while, and I found myself fighting to not believe it. I don't know why, but those feelings passed, and in time I was okay with it. Maybe I was just having a negative reaction because I was so overwhelmed with this new realization about myself. There's one thing I have to say. I know I've mentioned it several times in my writing that I was pissed off or angry or frustrated or I just wanted the whole damn thing to be over, but it's okay to have those feelings. An awakening isn't all fun and games. It's a very intense experience. Anyway, back to the topic of old souls. I certainly had to admit that I had the traits of an old soul, and that resonated with me on a very deep level.

I was thinking a lot about what I'd learned about myself and about what old souls were too. I was always different and never really like everybody else. I mean, I wasn't like creepy different, but I never really fit in with any cliques in school or at work. I tried to fit in, but I couldn't hide the fact that I was different. It just showed in everything I did and said, and I couldn't help it. To be honest, after trying for so many years, I really just didn't give a shit anymore, so I just stopped trying. It never felt right to not just be myself anyway.

It would always amaze me that people couldn't see what I see and pick up on things I could pick up on, and I could tell they couldn't. I've been dealing with that my entire life, and it turns out that's something that old souls deal with too. What a shocker, just like when I found out I was an indigo, I've got all the traits of an old soul too.

This was the second piece of my spiritual puzzle that's been made known to me, but why? I keep asking myself that question. I've discovered that there is so much more to me than I ever could have imagined. There've been many times during this experience that I've felt pissed off, irritated, frustrated, and downright depressed too, but there are also many times that I've felt so calm and at peace with myself. I can't remember ever feeling like that before all this began. I keep thinking I must be stronger than I ever thought I was because there's no way I would've made it this far if I wasn't.

Well, weeks turned into months as I went about my everyday routine of working and being a dad and being a husband. I was trying to just be normal, which for me isn't easy to do. I might have looked the same on the outside, but inside I was a mess. I wasn't sure who or even what I was anymore. I'd go from happy to depressed and from feeling calm to feeling anxious all in the same day. Hell, it could happen all in one hour sometimes. It was mentally exhausting.

I've seen artists who can draw optical allusions. The one I'm thinking of is a drawing of these steps. The way they're drawn—when you look at them, you can't tell if they're going up or going down; and the longer you look at them, your brain starts flipping the drawing. One second it seems like they're going up, and the next it seems like they're going down. That's how I was feeling. I didn't know if what was happening to me was good or if what was happening to me was bad. The more I thought about it, the worse it was sometimes. Back and forth I went. Yes, it's good. No, it's not. Yes, it's good. No, it's not. Just like the drawing, I didn't know which way I was going!

This experience was consuming me. I thought about all the stuff I found out about myself all the time. Over and over and around and around I went. At times it helped me feel more complete and more centered, but I knew there's more to it than that. That's what was driving me nuts. A lot of the time I felt the answers were right there on the tip of my tongue, yet they eluded me.

One morning I went out for a jog, which I started doing right after this all started. This particular morning wasn't any different from any other morning except for one thing. A thought popped into my head, but not just any thought. I had this thought in my mind, and it was very simple and to the point. There wasn't anything abstract about it at all. Basically, the thought was this. I had to experience my life exactly the way I did because if I didn't, I wouldn't be who I am now, and I wouldn't be able to do what I came here to do. That made sense to me, but selfishly, I would've preferred another way.

I was experiencing this awakening, which I still didn't understand at the time that's what the hell was happening to me. I was at the point in my awakening where I could tell whether or not I had a particular thought or if it was put into my mind as if it was imprinted there, by who or what, I didn't know at the time. I just knew the difference because those thoughts just felt different. It wasn't that I acquired some magical skill to know this. There's nothing magical about what's happening to me. I just know things and can feel things, and I can't explain completely how or why.

Throughout this whole experience I've felt conflicted inside. The ranges of emotions I've felt have swung from one end of the emotional spectrum to the other. Look, I was very happy and grateful to be alive. I was so excited to find out I was an indigo and an old soul too, but I couldn't help but feel frustrated because I didn't see the point. I just kept thinking, *I'm so old. What good is it going to do me now?* It blows me away how naive I was.

What was it I'm not getting? How is this going to help me? I'm just feeling more and more cut off from everybody and everything the more I progress through this experience; and to make things even crazier, if that's even possible, the more I find out about myself, the less I seem to understand. I'm just going 'round and 'round like I mentioned before, and I'm not feeling the kind of clarity I thought I would've by now. It's been several years, and I don't know where my thoughts are. I don't really know what I think about anything anymore. I just found out over the last couple of years some really profound stuff about myself, and yet I don't know how I feel about it. How can that even be? What is the end game? Where is this all going? I get a few answers, and then *wham*, ten more questions pop up.

This stuff doesn't happen to people in real life. I'm not special. I'm dreaming. I have to be. Every time I think maybe I could go talk to a psychiatrist about my situation, I quickly come back to my senses and realize there isn't one person that I can tell or talk to about any of this stuff. If I did that, they'd throw me in a straitjacket, have me heavily medicated, and then tossed into a padded room so fast my head would spin. This is clearly something I must go through on my own, and if that's the way it has to be, then so be it. I gave up and quit on myself once before, shame on me, but I'll be damned before I ever quit on myself ever again. I don't care what life throws at me. I know there's a lot that I don't know about what I'm going through, but I do know this. I'm going to see whatever is happening to me to its conclusion. I'm right here right now, and I'm going to become whatever it is I came here to be.

CHAPTER 6

And Down I Go...

At this point now in my journey, I'm so far down the rabbit hole there's no climbing out; but I guess even if I could climb out, I wouldn't now. My mind's made up. I'm going to see this thing through to its end. So I guess I'm going deeper down the rabbit hole, looking for the other side to come out of and hoping as I do that, there is another side to come out of. If there is, then I'll find it. That much I know. I'm on a journey within to understand my deepest self and to actually delve into my very soul.

It's been such an emotionally draining ride, but I don't care anymore because I've gone so far down the rabbit hole I've found out some really cool things and awesome stuff about myself so far. I truly have been blessed from the knowledge I now possess. I'm sure as hell not the same person I was just a few short years ago before this all started, and I know that I'm not yet the person I'm being led to become either. It's that gut feeling that tells me there is an end to all this. I just don't know when or where the hell it is, but it's out there. One of the coolest things about knowing and understanding what I know about myself now is just how it's changed my perspective of this reality. I mean on everything about this reality. I can't see anything the same anymore, but I like it! This new perspective feels strangely comfortable to me.

One of the changes that my wife has noticed is how much more confident I am. She mentioned it one day, and it really blow me away because my wife isn't one to give me complements about anything. It's just not her way. All the other changes I've hidden from her and everybody else that I know. What I mean is, I purposefully don't talk about my experience, and I go out of my way to not say things that would seem out of place or strange in any given situation that comes along—whether it's in my personal life or at work. This is my very own personal experience. It's just really weird to have this experience right under the nose of everyone you love.

I would contemplate for hours on how knowing and understanding I'm an indigo, an old soul, and an empath really helped me in this life. I feel more complete now, but I have to admit, coming to grips with the information I've learned took a lot more time and energy than I ever could've imagined. Don't get me wrong. I'm not complaining. It's just such an emotional thing sometimes it just sucks the life right out of me. Sometimes I wonder if just being a guy having to live life after almost killing himself would've been easier to deal with and accept than to have to come to grips with some of the crazy stuff this experience has been throwing at me.

Sometimes I think of myself now as well… weird, but in a very cool, cosmic, and spiritual kind of a way. I learned I was an indigo, and that led me to discover I was an old soul, which led me to understand that I was also what they call an "empath." Empathy is the uncanny ability to be able to understand and share the feelings of other people, but in a much-more-intense way. All this understanding has helped me answer a lot of questions about myself. Every time I learn something about myself, I get that rush, that beautiful rush, and it makes me feel so alive. Everything I learn puts a little piece of me back together. It makes enduring the pain of this whole awakening experience worth it!

I'll tell you what's crazy. I could really relate to that dude called Humpty Dumpty. He and I have a lot in common because we both had lots of pieces of ourselves to be put back together! The only difference between us was, he had all the king's horses and all the king's men to put him back together, and I only had myself.

This experience has given me the opportunity to know and understand myself in a way that most people can't even imagine, and I don't mean in a physical way. It's a very deep, spiritual understanding that I'm talking about. I feel special, and I don't say that in a bragging kind of way. The thing is, the deeper I go within myself, the more knowing and understanding I acquire, the more connected I feel to what I call the "divine presence" or what most people call God. I'm beginning to see the simplicity that hides within all the complexity of everything, from something as small as a blade of grass to something as big as this whole reality I live in.

All the downloads and imprints I receive I'm processing better now, which helps, but I still have a lot of crap in my head, and I still was struggling with not knowing what the hell was happening to me. It can't just be dumb luck that I never found out earlier that I was experiencing an awakening. That was being kept from me at that time, but I didn't know why. It's funny too because I'd learned so much, yet that still had alluded me.

Even with all this clutter in my mind, I still would hear that "something" telling me, "There is no going back, Ryan." I heard that thought a lot. One time, when I heard that thought, I got angry. I got really angry. I started yelling at that "something" that I heard. I was so frustrated. I weaved together tapestries of profanity that rivaled anything ever spoken! I got angry because I felt that I wasn't given a choice about any of this stuff, and I thought if there is no going back, at least I should be told where the hell I'm heading to! It's like I was blindfolded and told to go over there, but I didn't know where the hell over there was. There were many times during this experience that I would feel sorry for myself. I'd get over it, but I'd think how hard life is for me on a so-called normal day, and I just didn't need all this craziness going on in my mind all the time.

I want to say again that an awakening is an incredibility beautiful thing, to be sure, but it isn't all blue skies, rainbows, and tangerine dreams.

There are a lot of growing pains that go along with it. At least there was for me. I had to face a lot of painful truths about myself that I didn't like. Maybe because I didn't find out right away I was going through an awakening or maybe because I was so broken inside, I struggled more than most people would've, I'm not sure of the reason, to be honest.

Sometime later, after all this started, I took up jogging. I don't know why the thought or idea of it just kept popping up in my mind, so I did. It turned out there was something about jogging that I really liked. It relaxed me, and when I was jogging, it felt like my mind would open up. I could hear that "something" in my mind very clearly when I was jogging. As it turned out, I soon would find out that the "something" I heard in my mind was my higher self. It's like my body and mind would get in sync with each other when I was jogging. When that happened, it was like a vibrational key that would unlock and open up a part of my mind—a part of my mind I had no consciousness awareness of.

I remember I was jogging one day. I would go out in the early mornings because it was much cooler at that time of the day. Summers in Georgia were incredibly brutal because of all the humidity. I began noticing right away, when I did this, I would receive most of my downloads at that time. Remember downloads are just snapshots, memories, ideas, and thoughts that I would receive. It's just easier to say downloads, that's all. I didn't know if it was because of the time of day or the activity itself or a combination of the two, but that's how it was working out for me.

If anybody would've been around that morning I was jogging, they would've thought I was batshit crazy for sure! I found myself in a very strange and in an awkward situation even though I was all by myself at the time. It was the first time I realized I was talking out loud. I wasn't internalizing this conversation I was having when I was talking to the "something" in my mind. Even though I was by myself at the time, it just felt weird. I do it all the time now, but at that time, it was a new realization for me. I remember thinking how many times before I had been talking out loud and not even realized it. Crap, that's a scary thought, and how long had this been going on without me even being aware of it? Have I been even more out of it than I was afraid I was? I remember thinking, *I know I'm crazy, or I sure as hell am going crazy.*

Then something happened that was really strange. I know it's hard to believe that something really strange happened to me, but it's true. It had never happened to me up to this point. To say it blew me away is a fucking understatement! The "something" in my mind answered me. I'd always heard it before in my mind, but this time, I mean it interrupted me and responded to my outburst I was having. In the middle of my temper tantrum, I heard it clear as a bell, and it said, "You're stronger than you can imagine, Ryan," but I sure as hell wasn't feeling really strong at that time during all this, I can tell you that.

Now, I don't understand how, but understanding isn't always as important as knowing, but I knew in that moment in that instant that the "something" that interrupted me was my "higher self." Why or how, I don't know, but that thought, that very concept, was foreign to me at the time, and yet there it was in my mind. As soon as I had that thought, I got the biggest rush I've had yet. My eyes teared up so badly I could barely see where I was jogging. I knew it was the truth, and I realized I just experienced another "knowingism."

Looking back, I also knew why I'd been getting the urge to start jogging too. I needed to get to a higher vibrational state to connect with my higher self. My higher self was having too much interference from my ego, and this was going to change all that. I no longer refer to jogging as jogging anymore. I know that sounds stupid, but give me a minute.

Now I refer to it as my "physical meditation" because that's really what the hell I'm doing when I jog. It's all about body and mind and breathing. Sounds a lot like meditation to me! I could be wrong, but I think I just coined another new term. "Physical meditation." I like it, but we'll see. Time will tell.

The voice I heard in my mind the entire time ever since this whole experience began was a part of me. It was me, but just a higher version of me, that's all. That's why I was receiving most of my downloads when I jogged. It was because my mind was more open, and it was more open because I was resonating at a higher vibrational state. My higher self was then able to send a lot more information through to my lower conscious mind without the interference of my ego and its minions.

I think when I first was receiving downloads, my higher self would have to really cram what it could through a very small vibrational bandwidth. That's why in the beginning the information seemed so jumbled up to me. It's like trying to separate stuff that's in a box, but the box is so small, and there's too much stuff in the box, so everything just keeps running together as you try to separate it. That's what was happening in my mind, but I think that's all over now.

After that experience with my higher self, I felt surprisingly calm and comfortable with it. I felt relieved because at least I wasn't just hearing voices like some crazy person would. I mean, I was just hearing one voice, so I'm not crazy, right? I have a lot to learn still about the "higher self," but finally, I found out something about what the hell is going on.

As much as that day was on my mind the following days and weeks, I had some other thoughts that were lingering in that space between my ears. I really felt the need to find out more about empaths for some reason. I already knew some stuff about them, but with so much information to process and work through, I just hadn't focused on it too much. So I decided it's time to do exactly that.

No doubt or surprise the idea was put in my mind for a reason by my "higher self," I'm sure. I started checking stuff out on the PC, but I finished with a game controller in my hand and my game console fired up with that app I've used before. My back isn't what it used to be, so sitting in front of a PC for hours just doesn't work for me anymore. Getting old is a bitch!

I dove headfirst into as much information as I could find about "empaths." I found out people with this gift take empathy to a whole new level, but at the time, I didn't know just how high that level was. I learned more about empaths, and I quickly realized that this ability affected so many aspects of my life. I came to understand I wasn't just a regular empath, if there even is such a thing, and I'm not just an "intuitive empath" either. No, I'm a "hypersensitive, intuitive empath." I know what you're thinking. Man, I've never heard that term before, and you'd be right because once again, I've coined another term. I do believe that's five now that I've coined. Damn, I'm on a roll! I know it's mind-blowing and incredible, but the hits just keep coming!

You see, your average run-of-the-mill intuitive empath—and I say that in jest, of course—has the ability to feel other people's emotions and understand them as well. This drains the intuitive empath, but over time they instinctively learn how to block or reduce these emotions and their energies from coming in so they don't get so drained. For me, though, I can't turn my gift off like other empaths can. That's why I consider myself to be a "hypersensitive, intuitive empath." Other empaths might see this as a weakness. I don't know if they do, and I don't care either. It's forced me to become much stronger with my gift. I can handle a lot of emotional energy coming into me now. It also just never felt right to shut it down.

There is a catch, however. I reach a point where I automatically shut down. In the beginning I would shut down without warning because I didn't recognize the signs. As time went on, I could feel a shutdown coming because I understood the energies within my body and what they were telling me now.

This heightened sense of empathy explains my core personality to a tee. All the downloads I've gotten have led me to some pretty cool facts about empaths and things that I can really relate to. For me, being an empath and also being a guy comes with a price because I'm seen by other men as being weak or girly, but nothing could be farther from the truth.

Empaths have a keen sense when danger is close. They feel divine energy at certain moments in life. They know when it's time to move on from events in their life. Also, public places can really drain their energy, and people tend to tell them their problems, which is one of the things that really drives me crazy because I don't want to know everybody's problems. God knows I have enough of my own.

These are just some of the traits that empaths possess. It's taken me quite some time to understand and accept that being an empath and having these traits isn't a curse but a blessing. It's just that there's times it doesn't feel that way.

There have been so many changes within me, and I know I am better for it, but some of the stuff is just so hard to internalize and to digest, but I guess that old saying holds true. "No pain, no gain."

CHAPTER 7

What Backup Plan?

I'm seeing things for the first time in my life, and I'm slowly becoming more comfortable with what I am. I no longer care about who I am anymore. That seems pointless to worry about or waste my time thinking about. To me, that deals with the physical aspect of me, whereas "what I am"—now that's a question worth contemplating because that deals with the spiritual aspect of myself.

The relationship I have with my higher self feels surprisingly comfortable; yet at the same time, it's the strangest thing I've ever experienced. I know my higher self is a guide to understanding and a guide to knowing what I am! I also know I don't feel so all along now that I know it exists. In one sense, I've become my own best friend.

Time marches on, though, and I've been slinging propane tanks for almost three years now, and it's starting to take its toll on my body. Over time all the weight I've lifted is beating the hell out of my back and shoulders. About twenty years ago I had lower-back surgery, and that has problems all its own. Now I'm having issues with discs in my neck, numbness in my feet, my shoulders making grinding noises when I move them, and I've lost a lot of strength in them too. They hurt like hell after a day's work. Someone told me it might be bone spurs. Hell, I don't know. I'm popping over the counter pain and anti-inflammatory pills like they're candy just to kill as much pain as I can before my next day's work.

I don't say anything to my wife. I don't want to worry her, but I know I can't do this job much longer. It's time I go to plan B. The only problem is, I don't have a fucking plan B right now. Winter's just around the corner, and I hope I can somehow make it through till spring. If I can do that, at least my daughter will have some sort of a Christmas. I don't want to lose my job during the holidays because I'm not able to perform the tasks needed to do my job. I don't need to tell you how much that would suck! I need time to figure some stuff out, and besides, spring would be a better time to look for work anyway for sure. I honestly don't know if I can make it though. I guess time will tell.

The conditioning my whole life is to always expect the worst possible thing to happen to me whenever there's a chance; things could go either way. I just came to expect it. So there I was, thinking it's close to November, and I needed to make it to march, and there's no goddamn way that's going to happen. Then a thought occurred to me. Maybe I'd get lucky, and it'll be a mild winter this year. I've been out here for eight years and all, but one winter has been pretty mild, all things considered. Now I'm feeling better. I still got a chance. Not all hope is lost. Yeah, well, those happy thoughts lasted all of about six weeks before winter hit, and it turned out to be exactly what I was hoping to not have to deal with. That's just my luck, but it doesn't change the game plan because it's the only game plan I have. I've got to make it till spring.

There were many days during that particular winter in northern Georgia that I'd go to work and come home with frostbite so bad on my fingers they would just burn. At work, when I was handling the propane tanks, I would wear several pairs of gloves to insulate my hands from the cold tanks as best I could. Maybe it's old age, I don't know, but those tanks were so damn cold I'd pick them up, and their weight would press the ring handles up against my hands, and the metal tanks would suck the warmth right out of them. It didn't help that as I've gotten older, the circulation in my hands has gotten worse way worse in fact. I had to go out and buy one of those barbeque lighters—you know, the big ones—and keep it in my work truck. After I finished servicing an account, I'd have to grab the barbeque lighter and take my gloves off and hold the lighter under my fingers on both hands until I could get some feeling back into them. I'd get home after a long day, and my fingers would have black marks on them where they got singed from holding the damn lighter under them all day.

My wife noticed the marks on my hands and asked what they were. I didn't really want to tell her, but I was a horrible liar. I told her, and I could tell it kind of freaked her out. She couldn't believe what I was doing just to make it through a shift at work. Then she got curious, I guess, or maybe it was just good-old-women's intuition, but she asked me what else I wasn't telling her. She could tell I didn't want to really answer the question, so she started the conversation by saying she's noticed I've been taking a lot of the pain pills that were under the bathroom counter. She also noticed that I was walking slower and a little gingerly, so she asked if my back was also bothering me.

I said, "Yes."

Then she asked again, "Is there anything else you're not telling me?"

I thought about it for a minute and said, "Screw it."

I went ahead and told her about everything that I was having a problem with.

I told her, "My shoulders and my neck hurt. That my feet had numbness in them, and yes, my back is bothering me too." Everything hurts and aches, and I was having a hard time moving my head to the left side and lifting my shoulders above my head too. I told her I couldn't do this job much longer.

She just looked at me and said, "Do you think!"

That's why I love my wife. She doesn't pull any punches. She calls it like it is, and she just gets it.

I have to admit, I felt better telling my wife the truth. I didn't feel any better physically, but you know what I mean. I guess I just felt relieved that I didn't have to hide anything anymore. I guess I wasn't doing a very good job of that anyway. I don't even know why I thought I could hide this stuff from her. She always knew me in a way I never really understood. She said she's noticed for some time that things weren't right with me. I told her I just wanted to make sure Keanna, my daughter, had a good Christmas, and I didn't want her worrying either. It's all that mattered to me at the time. With everything happening to me and all this weird stuff going on, all I could think about was my daughter. I was not going to let any of my personal craziness affect her, period! She deserves as normal a childhood as I can give her. I owe her at least that much.

The winter came and went. I don't know how the hell I made it, but I did, and that's all that mattered. It's spring of 2015 now. My body's hurting so bad it's hard to even do simple, routine things around the house. It won't be long now before I can't physically do my job anymore. I had put off looking for another job all winter long. When you've basically spent your whole life looking for work like I have, the thought of having to do it again is just depressing, to say the least.

I woke up one morning, and I couldn't stop thinking about my résumé for some reason. To be more specific, I was thinking about the fact that I didn't even have a good updated résumé. The thought wouldn't leave my mind. It was Saturday, and like most Saturdays, my wife and I were going to be at my daughter's softball tournament all day. I always enjoyed those days because I could forget all my flipping problems for a while and just unwind. It gave me a chance to feel normal and just be a dad if only for a little while. I remember watching the games that day, but I was totally distracted. It was like the voice in my mind was saying over and over and over just to make a point, "Hey, what about your résumé? Hello, you know you got to get going on that."

The more I tried to focus on the softball games, the more thoughts kept flashing in my mind about my damn résumé, or lack of one. I was having all kinds of ideas about putting one together and what I wanted it to look like and what it should highlight about me and all that kind of stuff. I was getting very irritated, and eventually, I found myself talking out loud once again to my higher self, but this time I was sitting on the bleachers at my daughter's softball tournament. Not good because my wife could hear me.

She turned round and said, "You're talking to yourself again."

By now she'd gotten used to me talking to myself. I knew, however, if she heard me, then there were other parents that heard me too. Damn, I don't want this group of people thinking I'm batshit crazy. This is the only place I can go and not feel so different, and I might have just screwed that up!

My fear is that the other parents will say something to their kids about hearing me talking to myself, and they'll give my daughter a bad time or tease her about it. I don't want any of this stuff I'm going through to spill over into my daughter's life more than it already has.

The tournament came and went. I got up Sunday the next day and went jogging as usual, and the entire time I was focused on my résumé. It's all that was on my mind, of course. If nothing else my, higher self is very persistent. What a shocker!

I got home and showered and went up to my room jumped on the computer and went to work. I spent hours on it. I worked on it the rest of the morning and into the afternoon until it was done. I have no idea where all this motivation came from. I know where all the thoughts and ideas about the résumé came from, but not the motivation. I wonder if the thoughts, ideas, and images given to me carry with them an energy all their own that I don't yet understand. Maybe it somehow drove me to do what I did because I can tell you this, the last thing I wanted to do, especially on a Sunday, was to work on a damn résumé! Well, it's done, and that's a good thing, no doubt. It's not a bad thing at all that I worked on the résumé; it's just that I don't know why I did. It got me thinking. We say "we were inspired" when we do certain things in life, but where does that inspiration we feel really come from? It has to come from somewhere. I have my suspicions, but nothing concrete…yet.

It's funny how things work in my life now. You'd think I'd get used to it. Strange, but I never have, and it still kind of freaks me out. The next day I had off, so again for some unknown reason, I was "inspired," so I logged onto the unemployment website. I actually asked myself why I was doing this. I wasn't talking to my higher self this time. I was just talking to and asking my normal, conscious self if there is such a thing anymore. Look, I know what you're thinking, and you're right. This book just gets weirder and weirder as you turn the pages, but it's nothing compared to actually experiencing what I went through. Trust me on that.

I clicked on the tab that had the job listings and scanned down the page of the unemployment website. I was instantly drawn to an opportunity I saw for a "shoemobile driver/salesman." I read it, and I wasn't really sure if I had all the qualifications, but I thought, *What the hell?* I clicked on it, filled out the application and gave all the info needed, and attached my résumé. I looked at some other jobs, but in the end, that was the only one I applied for. I didn't give it much thought after that, and life went on.

It must have been a few weeks later I got a call. Now, by this time, I had all but forgotten about that job. So I called the person back, and we talked; and next thing I know, I'm scheduled for an interview.

"There will be a company representative in the Atlanta area on these dates, which one is best for you?" Because I work every other day, there was no conflict at all with my current job, so it was easy to schedule a day for an interview. When I got to the interview, I felt surprisingly calm. Maybe because I thought I didn't have a chance in hell to get the job. As it turns out, the company is based in Ohio, and the guy interviewing me was a big Ohio State Buckeyes fan, and so am I. We hit it off right away, and the interview went better than I could have ever dreamed of. Something told me, "This is your job." I just knew it. I remember thinking, *What are the odds?* The only job I apply for in three years, and *bam*, I just know it's mine. In the next couple of weeks, I did the drug screen and the physical while the company was doing the background check on me. Pretty routine stuff for a job nowadays.

The last couple of years I really wanted to leave Georgia. I just knew my time in Georgia was coming to an end. I don't know how I knew it, but I did. I was going to need a fresh start somewhere else, weird, because I felt a longing for a place I've never been to and didn't even know where it was or where it would be. It was a very strong feeling I had for some time now, but I had no idea where I would go or, more importantly, how I would pay for the relocation of my family. Plus, my wife and daughter really liked Georgia. Only thing is, if I get this job, I'm stuck here in Georgia, and that didn't feel right to me. I felt a little conflicted, but I knew my time in Georgia somehow, someway was coming to an end. I remember talking to my higher self about it on several occasions and not really getting any clear answers about it. No ideas or dreams or anything about it. It was really weird.

Finally, I get the call from the company's human-resources department. The call was brief, and the woman was straight to the point with no small talk at all. You could tell she's done this a hundred times before. Long story short: I didn't get the job. Before I knew it, I was hanging up the phone, and I was fucking devastated! I was in shock. I didn't understand. I knew that I was going to be working for that company. I felt it, I dreamed it and I had no doubt that this was the company I'd be working for. I didn't understand what the hell just happened. Ever since my awakening, I'd never been wrong when I have this strong of an intuitive feeling.

A few days went by, and the guy that interviewed me for the job left me several messages to call him.

My wife said I should talk to him, but I was like, "Why do I want to talk to him? I don't need him to tell me again I didn't get the job."

Finally, he left a massage that said something like, "Ryan, call me. We need to talk. It's important."

I don't know why, but I said, "What the hell," and called him.

He proceeded to explain to me why I didn't get the job. He basically said at the last minute, someone from inside the company applied for the job, and he had no choice. He had to hire from within the company first.

I said, "Well, that's great, but it doesn't really change anything."

He said, "That's where you're wrong. I would like to offer you a position as a fill-in driver/salesman."

I would be responsible for filling in for salesman all over the northeast and southeast as needed for a variety of reasons.

Then he said something to me I couldn't believe. He basically said that the company is expanding out west in about a year or so from now and will be looking for eight more drivers/salesman out there. I told him I'd be interested in one of the positions out west. I remember I was standing there in my kitchen. I had him on speaker phone, and he was talking and telling me about the company's plans, but I was lost inside my mind. I didn't know where my thoughts were. I just couldn't believe what just happened because things like this never work in my favor, but I was just offered a way out of Georgia.

Crazy. That's exactly what I needed to get out of Georgia. I know my wife and daughter didn't want to leave, but I knew it was going to happen because I'd felt it for some time now. I just didn't know how, but I did now. It's absolutely bazaar. I thought, *How is this even happening?* A lot of the time now I don't even feel like I'm in control of my life anymore, which wasn't really a bad thing, to be totally honest with you. It's not like I did such a great job of calling my own shots in life. What was hard to deal with at that time was, things were going much better for me now, but I was feeling like I'm the copilot in my own life! It's a very surreal feeling. What also was bothering me was, I found myself just waiting for the bottom to drop out and for everything to go to crap. That's how I was programmed to think my whole life, and breaking that programming was not an easy thing to do...at all! It took me years to finally break free of those negative thoughts.

I had conversations with my higher self about what was going on and asked all kinds of questions, but the only thing that came back to me was, I would know when I was ready to understand. I would get thoughts like these, and to me they sounded like something I'd read in a Chinese fortune cookie. God, I hated when I got answers like that from my higher self. It always irritated and frustrated me to no end.

I was given the weekend by the gentleman for the company to think the offer over. So I talked it over with my wife, and she understood. I need the job, we need the money, and my body couldn't do the propane gig anymore. Besides, from the day I interviewed for the job to the day, I was hired was about a month. I quit my propane job a couple of days after I interviewed. Not because I wanted to but because I was too physically beat up to do it anymore. So when I got the call and didn't get the job, I thought that's it. I'm completely screwed. I'm going to lose the house, and I didn't know what I was going to do. Then I get another offer from that company, and everything worked out even better than I could've ever imaged, but that month was still one of the longest months of my life. Waiting for that phone call was almost more than I could deal with. All I could think about was my daughter and how she was going to be affected if something went wrong. I don't think I've ever been so scared in my life, and I've been pretty damn scared before.

I say it a lot, but it was crazy. I was watching things falling into place and lining up in my life to help me get to where I needed to be to continue the journey I was on. I just knew that's what was happening, but I wasn't used to things going this well for me. The company would even pay for my family's moving expenses, and I was even going to make more money than I've ever made before. Consider my mind blown! I never could have imagined any of these things happening to me, but they did. Everything's been different for me since that day I had my breakdown. It wasn't easy to accept that maybe things were starting to work out a little better for me as of late because, you see, I'd spent my whole life crawling through roses and coming out smelling like shit! It's just something I seemed to be naturally really good at, unfortunately.

To use a computer analogy, as time went on, my entire thought process on everything—and I mean everything—was reformatted and upgraded to a higher state or level of consciousness within my mind. I no longer think about anything the same way. I don't look at any given situation the way I did before. It's impossible, and I couldn't even if I tried, but why would I want to? My old way of thinking led me to the bottle and bullet and almost to the end!

CHAPTER 8

It's Finally Revealed

"*I'm going through changes.*" Absolutely goddamn right! There's a song by a group named Black Sabbath, and in this particular song, there's a line that says exactly that. Those lyrics some up my life perfectly since my breakdown. It's like the song was written about me. Only thing is, the song was written in the early seventies, about forty-some years ago. I was only around seven years old at the time.

Time really flies when you're going through changes, I can tell you that, my friends. My moments of confusion and my moments of clarity come and go. It's like a beautiful symphony, an ebb and flow that washes back and forth in my mind and allows me to move ahead, but at a smooth and graceful pace that's not too fast for me. I've become aware of so much crazy stuff about myself in the last four-plus years it's really mind-blowing. Even with all these new revelations I've had about myself and the fact that I feel more whole or complete as a person, it isn't enough for me. In fact, it just feels like the beginning, really.

There's still something missing, and it's a big something too. I still don't know or understand exactly what it is that's happening to me. All these years later, and I still can't put a name to my experience. I believe, no, I know now that this information was withheld from me for the expressed purpose of the writing that I was inevitability going to be doing. I've never been told by my higher self what exactly is happening to me. I've only been helped along, guided, if you will, by it while I'm going through the experience. You see, not knowing the whole time what I was experiencing has given me an incredibility unique perspective on it. It forced me to truly have to commit and trust my higher self 100 percent, and by having to do that, I was having to trust in myself 100 percent, which is something I've never done or ever been able to do in my entire life.

I think of me and my higher self like this. In a road-rally race, there's a driver and a navigator. The driver has to trust his navigator completely to get them to the next checkpoint along the way. Obviously, it's the driver's job to drive or steer the vehicle, but it's the navigator's job to plan out and guide the driver in the right direction during the race, to let him know what signs to look for and to keep him at the right pace during the race they're experiencing. You don't want to get to the next checkpoint until the time is right because getting there too early could cause unforeseen consequences. Without the navigator, the driver would or could be totally lost and not even know it; and ironically, that's exactly how most people go through life—completely spiritually and consciously lost—and they don't even know it. It's not important for the driver to know how far to the finish line, only how far to the next checkpoint, and that's exactly what my higher self has been doing for me: pacing me, not letting me get to far ahead of myself, just guiding me to the next checkpoint I needed to get to. So much now makes sense to me. I had to learn this before I could learn that. I had to understand this before I could understand that. I had to know this before I could know that. That's how it worked.

I know and understand why I was so lost my entire life and the reason I always felt so broken up inside too. I was totally cut off and disconnected from my higher self. On a very deep level, now I can say I truly understand the fact that I was always searching for myself, and I never even knew it. I was driving blind, so to speak, and completely unaware of it too; and in my case, though, ignorance wasn't bliss. My ignorance almost killed me.

The realization of my ignorance was a very difficult one to accept, and this one really perplexed me for quite a few years. Even today, when I think about it, the first thing that pops into my mind is how much of my life I wasted; how much time I lost and I'll never get back. The range of emotions I feel when I'm contemplating this always amazes me. At times I felt like I let the divine presence down by not understanding earlier in life the things I know now. To be given this gift we call life and to squander it must surely be a sin if such a thing truly exists. I understand that I had to live the life I lived, and I know my life had to happen exactly the way it was, but it doesn't really make it easier to accept all those years I wasted. I don't think I'll ever be able to get over that. I think it's always going to be a thorn in the side of this whole experience, but I don't let those kinds of thoughts affect me in a negative way anymore, but they still linger.

I didn't know it, but the time had come for me to understand what the hell was happening to me. For me, that was the next checkpoint on my journey. Finally, I was going to know what I was experiencing. I guess my higher self figured it had taken me as far as I could go without knowing. It's a funny thing. I talk about my higher self as if it's another person or another entity. I guess I do because I'm always talking to it like it is another person or entity. It's hard for my lower mind to really comprehend what's going on in my head. My lower mind thinks it's really talking to another person probably because I usually talk out loud to my higher self when I am communicating with it. I've found out over these last few years just how limited and easy it is to fool the lower mind.

I feel like I'm moving to the next level of whatever it is I'm experiencing. I get the feeling there's more to know and more to understand. How much more, I don't know, but my intuition is much more attuned than it ever has been before in my life. I get intuitive rushes about things all the time now. I just know if something is or if it isn't. I'll let you think about what I just said for a minute. So when I say I have a feeling that there's more to come, I know in all that I am that there's more to come! I don't question my intuition anymore because it never misguides me.

Learning to trust my intuition says I trust in myself, and it's more than just believing in myself. It's knowing myself. That's something I've never been able to say my whole life, but I can now. "Knowing" is the key, not "believing," because knowing leads to truth, and the truth always sets you free.

One of the ways my higher self communicates to me is by giving me intuitive thoughts and feelings about things and situations that pop up in my life. It doesn't have to hit me in the head with a hammer anymore to get my attention, but it was definitely more effective than being subtle.

So it started. I began my day like most others. I headed out for some much-needed physical meditation, or jogging to normal people. I was talking nonstop to my higher self. I was just in that kind a mood that particular morning. I don't remember all what I was saying. I was in a good mood, and I literally was just rambling about all kinds of stuff. If you knew me, you would know that I tend to do that when I have a lot on my mind, and I did that morning.

I had a lot of mornings where I would do this, but this was going to be another one of those mornings that was going to be a little different because somewhere in the midst of all my rambling, I asked the question I needed answered the most, and this time was going to be the last time I'd have to ask the question—the question that's haunted me and hung in my mind like cobwebs high up in a corner just out of reach. For four long years I asked the question while speaking to my higher self and never got an answer. The only answer I ever got was silence on that subject, the kind of silence that could drive you mad if I let it; and if I hadn't been strong enough, it would've put me over the edge for sure. I wasn't even thinking about what I was saying that morning to my higher self, and before I knew it, I asked, no, I screamed, "Why don't you just tell me what the hell is happening to me?" The moment I asked the question I heard nothing. There was just silence in my mind. It was like the whole world went quiet.

All I remember hearing were the sounds of my feet hitting the pavement and my heart pounding as I did my physical meditation. I waited for what seemed like forever, and then *bam*! I had a download that was massive. It was like my mind was racing a thousand miles an hour with all kinds of thoughts, ideas, concepts, and visuals, just racing round and round in my head, but no answer to my question—to the question. I was not happy at all!

My morning ritual of physical meditation came and went, and I couldn't believe I didn't get some kind of an answer. I mean, for Christ's sake, anything would've been nice, but no, nothing! Things were quiet for a week or so, but I'd been having some really strange dreams since that morning, and I'd become more and more consumed with knowing what was happening to me and why I hadn't been led to that answer yet.

I was thinking about it all the time now. I was totally obsessing on it. I can't tell you how many times I was completely lost in thought, thinking about it. My wife or daughter would be talking to me, and I wouldn't hear them. I'd just see their mouths moving. It was really strange. It was like someone hit the mute button on both of them. It was actually kind of cool now that I think about it.

I knew my higher self was up to something, not saying anything and just letting me sort through all those downloads I received that one morning, but what that reason was, I didn't know.

There were so many of them I couldn't really concentrate on any specific one at all.

The more I thought about those downloads, the less abstract they became, though, but it took some time. My thoughts were getting more focused now, but they were still just really bazaar. I needed to know why my higher self was so quiet about the subject. I felt that was the key. I spent the better part of a day talking to my higher self, trying to get some answers, but again nothing. I wasn't really having any kind of a normal conversation with my higher self because I was the one doing all the talking, and it wasn't saying anything!

Later that night I was sleeping and dreaming as usual. I remember I was dreaming about these babies. I'd been having this dream ever since that day I asked the question that final time. I'd been having this same repetitive dream all night long for days now. It's like it was just looped over and over and over as I slept. I was looking at all these newborn babies, and they were all sleeping and waking up, and that's all they were doing. There were hundreds of them. I remember thinking in my dream how cool it is that they're seeing things for the first time and everything they see will be known to them in a brand-new way. I remember thinking in my dream how that rocks and feeling so happy for those babies.

Then one morning, after waking up from the dream, *bam*, there was the answer. It must have been about three in the morning, but hell, I couldn't sleep. I walked very quickly upstairs to my "don't screw with me now" room and jumped on my app to check some stuff out. I was pretty jacked, to say the least. It was tattooed right in the front of my mind. I'm having a spiritual awakening, and it's causing an expansion of consciousness too! I remember saying, "Holy shit! Those are real?" Like those babies in my dreams, I'm seeing things for the first time, and all things will be made known to me. Wow! Now I was really rushing, and my whole body felt electric. My eyes were watering again, and my emotions were all over the place now.

Now I know why my higher self didn't tell me because it knew I needed to discover this on my own. It knew what the impact that discovering this myself would have on me. My higher self knew, and that's why it didn't tell me. Son of a gun, I can't believe I didn't figure it out sooner. Seriously, it's just another moment I had during this whole experience that had me feeling very humbled.

It was surreal all this time. I've been wondering, asking, and wanting to know what the hell was happening to me these past four-plus years, and then the answer came to me like this. It just never dawned on me. Well, I'll be dipped! You mean to tell me, all I had to do was start having some crazy dreams about babies, and *bam*, there's the answer. Are you kidding me!

Only in my life could something like this happen. I remember thinking how anticlimactic it all felt to me. I recall saying to my higher self, "Really, that's it? That's how you're going to reveal the big question to me, through a crazy dream about babies?" This should've been my big moment. I should've been ecstatic and so happy I could just shit, but instead I found myself conflicted with the feelings of frustration and disappointment about everything. It seemed like I'd been robbed of my big moment. I'd been through so much and endured and learned more than I ever could have imagined over the past four years. I just thought I deserved more. Looking back now, I understand that was just my ego talking at the time.

I couldn't see it at the time, but there was a process going on during my awakening. That's why my higher self was silent and wouldn't tell me anything. I had to find out for myself. It's all been part of a spiritual flow I've been going through. There was a reason why everything was happening the way it was happening during this whole experience. My awakening has been a very mind-blowing ordeal. The whole thing is ironic because the more I learn, the more I understand how much I don't know; and that may be the most profound thing I've ever said in my whole flipping life, and I'm not kidding either. Maybe I am getting a little wiser after all.

Well, the cat's out of the bag, and I could only think of one thing to do now. So I jumped on that app and dove into trying to find out all I could about what an awakening was. I just always kind of thought spiritual awakenings only happened in the movies, not in real life. I thought that's Hollywood stuff, and if someone thought they were going through one, then they were probably just a little nuts. I know now what an awakening is in one sense because I've been experiencing one, but I wanted to see and hear what others were saying about the subject. I knew that I was going through something strange, but I hadn't got to the point where I was thinking that others might be going through what I was too. Why would I think others might be experiencing something that I believed to be fantasy? I was so consumed with my experience and what I was discovering about myself I didn't even think about others out there that may be experiencing the same thing. Hell, half the time I thought I was just going crazy, losing my damn mind.

I understood more about what an awakening is after hours upon hours of research and watching other people's testimonies about their experience, but what really blow me away was that I found out I was part of a much-bigger awakening that was happening throughout the world. A mass awakening, if you will, but there's a very powerful truth that came along with my awakening. I had to come to grips with the fact that everything I thought I knew to be true was bullshit! The world I thought I knew has been completely turned upside down to me right now. I don't think that will ever change. The truths I accepted my whole life were really all lies, but I'm not alone. There are more and more people like me out there, people who are waking up and coming to know the true nature of this reality and also the true nature of what they are.

I know that indigos like me are light workers and that there are other light workers out in the world too. Some of them are star seeds, crystal children, and rainbow children. I know there are many more out there, but I've only learned of these few at the present time.

The anger I felt about how I found out what was happening to me passed. The more I thought about it, anger was just another knee-jerk reaction to this whole experience. I wasn't really mad at my higher self, and I came to the point where I felt guilty for being pissed off and yelling at my higher self. What's really crazy, though, is my higher self is just a more-consciously aware version of me. So I guess you could say I was just yelling at myself. That really messes with my head when I think about it.

It's all just so weird; yet at the same time it makes total sense to me. I don't know what that says about me. I just find myself talking about my higher self as if it's another person or entity, which to me has become totally normal, and yet it still sounds crazy, but that's how it is. I know and accept what's happening to me, but I'd be lying if I said it doesn't freak me out sometimes, and till this day there are times when it all just blows me away. I look at my life the way it is now, and it's so different from how it was before.

Finding out that I was experiencing an awakening after finding out that I was an indigo and an old soul and a hypersensitive, intuitive empath was a lot to deal with and process in my mind. I mean, four years ago, I just thought stuff like this happened to other people—if it happened at all—or hell, maybe just in the movies. Something tells me there's more to come, and that's become the real story of my life now. I don't know what the future holds. I don't know why I was spared that fateful day all those years ago. I don't know why I'm not dead right now. I don't know what keeps me moving forward. I don't know how I've endured these past years with all this craziness going on in my mind, and I sure as hell don't know where this is all going either. With that said, there's one feeling that hangs over me and looms over everything that's happened for me, and it's the extreme feeling of isolation. It's always there, and I know it always will be.

There's just this feeling in my heart and this knowing in my mind that gets me through to another day. There's a light and an energy that radiates inside me that I never felt before, but it's always been there. I know it. I just wasn't aware of it before because I was so broken apart spiritually and consciously my whole life. I was totally asleep, just sleepwalking through day after day after day. When I look into the mirror, I see this light in my eyes. I call it the "shine," and yes, that's another new term I came up with. Thank you very much! This "shine" that I see in my eyes now is a gift. It's a mark of sorts. I see it in my eyes, and I see it in other people's eyes too; and when I notice it in other people's eyes, they always seem to have a certain energy that I pick on from them.

When I think I can't go on anymore, I feel an energy pulling and pushing me on. It's a different type of energy than the energy rush I described earlier in my writings. It almost feels angelic in nature, and it calms me and gives me strength. I find myself actually looking forward to waking up in the morning now to see what the day will bring. I spent most of my life always dreading the next day to come. Those days are over, and I don't know what tomorrow will bring, but I'll be there to experience it.

CHAPTER 9

The Way It Has to Be

An awakening—what the hell! Now that I know it really does happen to people, and it's not just a Hollywood movie thing, aren't awakenings the kind of thing that only happens to monks, priests, and people of that stature, only for people that are worthy of such a spiritual experience? I guess not because I'm living proof that isn't the case. I'm just as special or worthy as any priest, king, or president that exists in this reality. Those are just titles we bestow on people, nothing more. It didn't matter who I was or what my status in life was or how much money I made. I still experienced this awakening. It was something incredibly beautiful and terrifying all at the same time. I have to tell you, for just an average guy, I feel kind of special in a strange, cosmic kind of way. I feel like I was chosen, but the question lingering in my mind is, by what or by who?

Before this entire awakening ordeal started, I would've told you that it was God or maybe even the devil messing with my head. I obviously was either being punished by one or deceived by the other, but now I know that's not true. Most of my old, conditioned ways of thinking are gone now, but I still struggle because, after all, I had over four decades of conditioning to undo. That's a lot of rewiring to go through and sort out. Now I have these intuitive thoughts that say either I chose to have this experience or some higher power chose for me to have it. Either way, the end result is the same. Did I choose to incarnate here in this realm we call Earth and experience everything I experienced? Whether I'm right or wrong about it, it wouldn't change the fact that my experience or my awakening—whatever you like to call it—happened. My whole life played out like there was some cosmic hand at work in all of it. I went from one experience to another all the while each one was moving and pushing me closer and closer to the day I'd eventually begin my awakening, like a piece of clay being molded and shaped into form by every event that I ever experienced. Looking back on it now, if it was me, it was one crazy plan; and sometimes when I think about it, I'd like to kick my own ass for planning the way it all went down, but I guess it all worked out in the end. I'm still here, and I'm talking about it.

On the other hand, if it was by divine intervention, then that opens up a whole other avenue of possibilities to be considered. I have this wild thought. What if being a soul makes me divine in nature? What would that mean? I think it would mean that I truly am responsible for everything that happens to me; that on some level of consciousness, I control all that I experience regardless of how good or how bad those experiences might be. That in and of itself is a great gift and a great responsibility too. That means that I am the sum of all that I experience. All the time now I have thoughts about whatever it is I'm thinking about, and I find myself wondering where those thoughts are coming from. I know that I'm tapped into something—something so huge in magnitude—and I've felt it throughout this whole experience, but what that something is, I'm not a hundred percent sure of…yet.

I was systematically being broken down with my life experiences just like a marine sergeant who gets a new group of recruits and breaks them down so they can build them back up in the marine way of thinking and doing things. I was going to be built back up with true strength, spiritual strength not physical strength. I guess it's the closest thing to being what religious people call "being reborn." It's ironic because as I was being broken down throughout my life, I was also gaining the strength I would need to make through this whole awakening experience once it began. To me that just reeks of intelligent design. In fact, I see intelligent design everywhere I look. Whether I'm looking at something in this world or looking within myself, its mark is always there for those who have the eyes to see it.

I was going to need to be stronger than I could imagine, and living through all the crap I experienced during my life gave me that inner strength. Like I just said a moment ago, I was slowly being broke down over the years with all my unfortunate experiences and also gaining the strength I would need for things to come. It helped me acquire an inner strength, one I never would've gotten if I lived a life with a silver spoon up my ass. I see that now. I see so much now that I couldn't see before. It's truly one of the things I'm most grateful for. The perspective I have on things now is just awesome, but it's also kind of freaky too. I get very emotional, and tears stream down my face when I think about how far I've come. I'm beginning to have a sense of pride and a growing sense of peace about who and what I am that I never felt before, and it feels really good.

I still don't have a lot of money or a big house or a new boat or a new car, and I really don't care because what I'm feeling growing inside me is priceless and eternal. You never lose what you gained from experiences during a lifetime spent in this realm even though when you incarnate here, you can't recall past lessons learned, but that's only for a brief time. Once you cross back over, all is made known to you again.

When you've been as lost, broken, and separated from yourself as I was for so long, living a life without any sense pride or peace, it breaks you down. Day in and day out I basically lived in fear of this or fear of that and fear of the next day to come, and then one day to finally have feelings that were positive feelings and also have this light grow inside me feels just awesome! I couldn't have gotten to that point if not for the experiences that I put myself through. I know for most people out there, that's going to be a very tough concept to wrap their mind around. I still find it hard to believe, but I'm pretty sure that's exactly what was going on during my entire life. Everything that ever happened to me was self-inflected.

When I found out what was happening to me, I had a lot of conversations with my higher self about the process. I had so many questions about all of it. Why this and why that about every aspect of my awakening. I've always talked to my higher self as if it was another entity within me. I guess in one sense, it was; and in one sense, it still is. Since this all started, I've talked more to my higher self than any other human being that I know. I'm fully aware of how that must sound to people, but for me it's become perfectly normal. Back a few years ago, the waters of my life were a lot muddier than they are now. They've gotten much clearer, and I have a greater understanding of my experience now; but hell, I have a greater understanding of everything about myself now.

My higher self guided me to discovering what was happening to me. When I finally found out I was far enough along, I understood that this awakening and everything I've experienced wasn't happening to me but happening for me. That's a big difference in thought and perspective. I just knew that was the truth of it, but it took me years to really understand what that meant, like so many other things that I just know now. It's all part of this experience. However, my higher self wasn't ready to just give me insight into my awakening or the process I was going through. I had to figure that out as I went, and I did, but it took time and experience to do it.

I was always reflecting back on my life now, and when I did, certain experiences would stand out and come forward in my mind. I spent a lot of time thinking about those memories. I knew there was a reason for a particular memory to come forward, and it was always to teach me something or to help heal me in some way spiritually. I was replaying these memories over and over in my mind, and I was reliving them emotionally. The good memories were easy to experience again, and they reminded me that my whole life wasn't all bad and definitely not a waste either. The bad ones, however, were intensely horrible to have to relive again. How do I explain the mental and emotional draining that happened to me while I relived all these past experiences, especially being a hypersensitive, intuitive empathy like I am! It was a very difficult thing for me to do, and I had to do it a lot over the years during my awakening. Knowing and understanding weren't enough for me. I also needed a tremendous amount of spiritual healing. All those things took a lot of energy and time to accomplish.

I understood what these experiences did for me know, especially the bad ones, because they healed me. I got to the point where I embraced the memories of my bad experiences in my life more than the good ones because they were the ones that also gave me my inner strength—strength I covet so dearly till this very day. I reflected on those memories all the time. It's hard to say just how much time I spent because time was moving so quickly for me now. I understood know what my higher self wanted me to learn and to know and understand. I realized it was just as important to accept all the decisions and consequences that came from my bad experiences as it was to accept the decisions and consequences of the good experiences as well. I can't say it enough: you are the sum of everything you experience in this reality.

All experiences are either positive or negative, opposite sides of the same coin, connected to one another in some beautiful, cosmic way I don't yet fully understand. Funny thing is, neither of them can exist without the other. Above all else, you must have balance within your mind. There is no light without darkness. You can't just pick and choose what experiences you want to make you who you are and to define yourself. That's a big part of the reason I felt so broken up inside. I wasn't accepting all of what I was but only part of what is was. That was a very important lesson I had to learn during my awakening. I can't stress enough how that understanding has helped me become more complete.

Out of the blue, one night my higher self said to me in so many words, "What you just discovered and learned about yourself was the purpose of your life, Ryan. You incarnated here to go through this process because it was your time." It took me by surprise. I'm not sure why anything surprised me anymore, but it did. I was surprised because it never said things to me that were so direct before. I was also surprised, I guess, because my higher self had been quiet for some time before that night. Once again, it was giving me time, letting me process and finally accept a lot stuff I needed to sort out and work through.

What I learned and came to understand about the first forty-four years of my life before my awakening began was mind-blowing. Once I learned that the purpose of my life was all about preparing myself for my awakening that would eventually come, I felt a sense of relief, and that gave me a sense of peace inside. I remember thinking how those forty-four years damn near killed me, or should I say, I damn near killed myself! My emotions were all over the place, going every which way, and sometimes I felt very conflicted when I thought about what I had learned and now understood about my past. It was overwhelming at times. Will there ever be an end to all of this? That's a thought I often had during my experience. Where is this all going?

Then I had another thought. If there is an end to all this, then just how long can this awakening last? The thought of that at the time scared the crap out of me. I figured if it took me forty-four years of living to be ready for my awakening, then my awakening could possibly last for a long time too, and that thought wasn't one that gave me happy, happy, joy, joy feelings, if you know what I mean. Look, I know that my awakening was a really good thing, and let's face it, that's obviously a massive understatement because it's by far the best thing to ever happen to me, but let's be honest; the first few years of this experience was no picnic—not even close to it—and not knowing how long it was going to last didn't exactly enhance the experience any and make me feel all warm and fuzzy inside.

I tell you, there are a lot of things you have to deal with after you begin the process of an awakening that aren't so fun. When you don't even know that you're going through an awakening like I didn't, it's even worse; but if I can make it through one, then you sure as hell can too! *You probably won't read another book about an awakening experience like this one. I just really wanted others to know that they're not alone, and if and when you begin to experience an awakening, just know it's worth all the pain.*

When I asked my higher self just how long will my awakening last, the first thought that popped into my mind after asking was, "How long will the sun shine?" I thought, *What do you mean, how long will the sun shine? That's not even fair.* That's a horrible answer for someone who's so desperate for answers. I see why now when I talk a lot of the time, I sound like a Chinese fortune cookie. It's because I've been listening to my higher self talk to my mind for years that same way. I guess it just rubbed off on me. I shouldn't be surprised it happened. I mean, I've spent so much time in conversions with my higher self over these past years.

I know that I'll know what I need to know when I need to know it. Now that's a mouthful to be sure. Damn it, I really hate when I get intuitive thoughts like that because I know they're right, but I don't like what they mean for me. During my awakening, my conversations with my higher self weren't always one sided, but I look back on it, and I understand why. At those times I was being allowed to know and understand in my own time and in my own way what the meaning of the first forty-four years of my life was and other things too, of course. That was so important for my spiritual growth and healing. It wasn't forty-four wasted years like I thought. There was purpose and meaning to all that time in my life. I know that was a very powerful thing for me to understand and, more importantly, to accept. I was carrying a lot of guilt and regret about those years. I thought I was just a loser and a failure and an underachiever, just drifting through life, void of any purpose whatsoever. The only purpose in my life was trying to survive day to day, and that's it. I was just so damn wrong about so much. I know I can never get all those years back, but that's why I'm more determined than ever to not waste what time I have left in this reality.

Think about this. I was going to end my life because of what I was experiencing during those last few years of my forty-four-year experience before my awakening began. I couldn't see anything good about those years, let alone feel there was any purpose to all of them. I've done a complete 180 on my perspective on how I view my past now. I was taught to believe in myself, but never was I taught to know myself. That's a very powerful realization, and it shows how much my perspective on life has changed. I don't think any of us are really taught that, and it's a shame. To know yourself is to understand what you truly are, and that's a game changer. I'm going to really dive into that topic in my next book, but what I will say is, this reality we live in would change dramatically if people understood the concept of "self."

It wasn't until later in my awakening that thoughts were coming to me when I was doing my physical meditations that were helping me connect the dots about my awakening process and what it was and why I hadn't seen or noticed it. I hadn't noticed it because things were coming at me so fast, and gee, it wasn't like I didn't have enough stuff to think about during that period in my life, but that's no excuse. It's just the way it was.

I understood I was led to discover all that I discovered during my journey, but for some reason, I didn't see the bigger picture. There was just so much new information to take in, and besides, learning those things about myself was overwhelming. I just needed time and lots of it too. I wasn't only learning new information but I was also contemplating what I learned and why I learned it. I was mentally drowning in thoughts and memories every day. I was also being hit with massive downloads about all sorts of stuff that was dealing with my past and really messing with my mind. Hell, it took me a while to even see and understand that everything I experienced in my life was connected and part of the process. I actually used to think my life was just a bunch of random events that happened when they happened. I can't believe I thought like that, but I did.

I always felt like I was just one of those people that was always going to get the short end of the stick in life. That way of thinking has a way of becoming a self-fulfilling prophecy. That's some really messed-up programming I did to myself. I look back, and I realize that I had become my own worst enemy. How crazy is that? This whole experience really messes with my mind. One day my thoughts were as clear as a blue sky, and the next day they were as cloudy as muddy water. One day you're happy, and the next day you're sad. This experience had taken me up, down, twisted me all around, and pushed me to my limits, but that was okay because I was finding out that I could be pushed a lot farther than I ever could have imagined.

Finally, though, I saw and understood the overall process of my awakening because of all the guidance and information that I'd received from my higher self over the past four plus years. It was finally coming together. It was 2015, and a lot of the mental grunt work was over. Now I was feeling the expansion of my consciousness and experiencing how much more aware I am and seeing how that has changed my perspective in ways I could've never had imagined. I realized that the past four years after my breakdown, I needed to be educated to learn some very important things about myself that would act as a foundation for what was to come next in my awakening. I also needed spiritual healing so badly it wasn't funny, and while all this was going on in my mind, the world around me was moving right along like it always has. I still had to do all my everyday things I did with and for my family. My wife and daughter went about their daily routines completely oblivious to what I was going through. I just felt like, surely, someone would notice something, but no, really, that never happened.

Another one of the weird things I experienced was that, on one hand, in my mind everything was going a mile a minute, and you're just freaking out and feeling like you're coming apart at the seams, but at other times in my mind it seemed like time was slowed down and just crawling at a snail's pace throughout my awakening. I really had no concept of time for quite a while during this whole experience.

I think about it now, and I break my awakening down into three stages. Each stage had several steps that I had to go *through and experience. The first stage of* the process was all about self-educating. That started right after my breakdown. This one was hard for me because I was so ignorant to what I was experiencing at the time. It was teaching me about myself and opening my eyes to help me see how these discoveries of being an indigo, an old soul, and an intuitive empathy were the reasons I did what I did, acted the way I did, and thought the way I did my entire life. They were what made me who I was.

It was a very slow process, but it had to be because of my mental and emotional condition at the time. I was very fragile and a completely broken man. Like an egg, it wouldn't have taken much to break me; and if I would've broken down again, I don't think I ever would've recovered.

The second stage of the process was all about self-healing. This stage ended up having five steps I identified and each one building on top of the other. I began experiencing this stage a year or so into my awakening. It was somewhere around that time after many conversations with my higher self that It must have felt I was ready to move on to what I now understood was that second stage. This one was difficult because I was going to have to face myself. My real self! Not the self my ego had created. I guess my higher self felt I had the inner strength I'd need to face myself all of myself, not just the good but the bad too. I, however, would be lying if I tell you I didn't have some reservations about it. To be totally honest, I was scared, but at the same time I was strangely curious and eager to experience whatever was in store for me. I guess somewhere deep inside me I knew it was time to move on.

The third and final stage began in late spring or early summer of 2018, however you want to look at it. This stage was by far the most challenging for me because this stage was a whole new animal to have to deal with! It was all about transformation, and I'll get into *that later on. I really just want to focus on the first two stages for the time being.*

In the first stage of my awakening, there were four steps I experienced in a very precise order, and there wasn't anything random about what I went through either. First, I want to tell you about a very simple concept and a very important concept to wrap your mind around and to understand. This thought popped into my mind, and when it did, I realized that everything wasn't happening to me but instead it was all happening for me! When I came to this understanding during my journey, it changed my whole perspective of my experience. After that happened, it was much easier to deal with all the crap that was being thrown at me. When I thought or felt like something was happening to me, I saw that and interpreted that as a negative thing; but when I thought or felt that something was happening for me, I saw that as a very positive thing for me. I wish I would've been seeing things from this perspective all along, but I always seem to find the hard way to do everything. I guess you could say it's just my way, slow and steady, but I guess that's not the worst way to go through life.

The second stage of my awakening had five steps to it. The first four steps were the same as the four steps in the first stage as it turned out. As I'm sitting here, thinking about what I'm going to write about the process and how I'm going to explain how it works or worked for me, I find myself thinking how beautiful it all was and just marveling at the pure genius of the whole thing.

This is how my whole awakening worked out. There was always a method to the madness, it seems, but I just wasn't privy to it. A big part of the whole experience for me was figuring out in my own way and in my own time what the process was and why it had to be that way. I had to come to my own conclusions and understanding of the experience I was going through. How I perceived my awakening would determine how I'd experience it and who I will become.

With that said, the first step in the first two stages was "learning." I had to learn about whatever it was I was receiving downloads about, and trust me, that was a lot of stuff to learn. Once I learned about something, that meant I now knew about it, and "knowing" was the second step. To truly know about something takes time. Once I learned about something and then came to know it, that would lead me to the third step, which was "truth." I would over time come to see the truth of what I came to learn and know. I'd spend hours talking to my higher self and contemplating information given to me. When I did finally get to the point where I saw the truth of something, then that led me to the fourth step, which was "trust," and thinking about it now it makes perfect sense. My higher self had it all planned out. I would be introduced to something a concept or idea, and I'd learn about it. Then I would come to know it, and eventually, I would see the truth of it. Once I'd gotten that far, it was only natural to trust what I had learned and what I now knew and saw the truth in. It didn't matter how long it took for me to get there. My awakening was never about time, at least not how we perceive it in the physical world. Time was an irrelevant concept to the process.

The fifth and final step was, by far, the most important. It's what came at the end of the second stage. The final step was to "heal." It's the reward I got for going through and experiencing and enduring this whole awakening ordeal. I was able to love myself for the first time in my life. I don't mean in a narcissist or self-centered kind of a way but in a truly self-accepting way. The way I got there was by letting go of my past and by accepting all that I had experienced. I mean really and truly accepting it with all that I am! How do I put into words what it's like to experience spiritual healing? The one thought that comes to mind is that I'm just completely satisfied and comfortable with who and what I am now. I'm no longer judging myself based on materialistic things that I have or don't have, and I'm no longer judging myself based on any materialistic accomplishments I've achieved or haven't achieved.

Everything is internal now, not external. It certainly wasn't an overnight process, but in time I began to feel a sense of calmness and peace come over me. For the first time in my life, I felt complete and not all broken up inside, but maybe I'm not done healing yet. I honestly don't know when or if that ever happens.

I understand because of the process I was put through that I have an inner strength and an inner light that will always be there. It was always there; I just couldn't see it. I do what I do because I am what I am. Until this awakening happened, I didn't know who I was or what I was.

Don't get me wrong. There was definitely a heavy price to pay, as there always is. It felt like I was going through hell to get to heaven, but it's okay because I'm at peace with myself and the world around me, and that's a very liberating feeling. It's changed me in so many ways. It's as if a dark veil has been removed from my eyes. "Where I once was blind, now I see." There are no words that ring truer for me than those.

CHAPTER 10

Never Say Never

There's an old saying that's really resonated with me more and more as I progressed through my awakening, and it was, "Never say never." Those are words I live by every damn day of my life now! As we go through life, we hear a lot of different "sayings" about this and that, but we never really give them much thought. I know I didn't even though I used them all the time in my day-to-day life.

Little did I know that the year 2016 was going to be a never-say-never kind of year. It started out as a pretty normal year, which is a very bold statement coming from a guy like me with all the weird stuff I've experienced in my life, especially in the last few years. I was still working for this national company selling safety shoes, and things were going as good as could be expected for me. My wife and daughter were doing just fine. My wife was working at my daughter's school in the cafeteria, and my daughter was well…just being a kid, and that was great! I was staying busy enough where I hadn't given any thought to what was talked about and agreed upon when I accepted this job close to a year ago, but that wasn't going to last for long. The only thing that was a little strange and, to be honest, quite surprising was the fact that my brother had separated from his wife and was getting a divorce after eighteen years of marriage, but you know what they say. "Shit happens." Does it ever!

I guess it was sometime in early February I started having thoughts popping into my head about my bother not living in Georgia anymore. I would have dreams, and in them I'd go over to his house, and he wouldn't be there, and I could feel he didn't live there anymore. I knew that was crazy to even think he would leave because he loved Georgia; yet the dreams and thoughts of it happening were there in my mind. I was thinking about what I would do if anything ever happened to my brother, and he did move or, for whatever reason, he wasn't there anymore, and how it would affect me.

I moved to Georgia in the first place partly because he was there, and I would visit him once a year, and I liked it. It appealed to me because of the situation I was in back in Oregon where I was living at the time. I was always in some kind of a messed-up situation. In fact, I spent my entire life just going from one screwed-up situation to another. You do it so long it just becomes the norm. How insane is that!

Anyway, I was having these thoughts and dreams of my brother for weeks. I would lose time and not remember what I had done or been doing because I was so deep in thought about it. Also, those dreams I was having at night were a little disturbing and didn't help matters either. They were just crazy dreams with my brother in them, and it seemed as if they would last all night long. I'd get up and go to the bathroom and go back to bed, and they would start up right where I left off in the dream.

The thing is, when I'd get up in the morning, I'd have this horrible, ominous feeling in the pit of my stomach that he was gone, and it would almost make me sick because the feeling was so intense. It was an awful, empty kind of feeling I felt in my heart like when someone you love dies. I didn't like it at all. The dreams left me with a really uneasy feeling, and these bazaar dreams went on for a while. It was getting to point that I didn't what to go to sleep because I didn't want to have of those horrible dreams anymore.

I was losing sleep, and I kept thinking that something bad was going to happen to my brother, and it scared the crap out of me. What else could these thoughts and dreams mean other than that? With all the weight of those thoughts and dreams and the feeling they left me with, I just knew something bad was going to happen to him, and it was tearing me up inside. Getting up every day, not knowing and thinking this could be the day was, in a word…terrifying.

My brother had separated from his wife some time in 2013 and had been living on his own for several years. He lived close to his kids. I know he loved them more than life itself. In a thousand years, I couldn't imagine him moving away; that's why I was convinced that my thoughts and dreams had to be about some kind of tragedy that was coming.

Even with all this confusion going on in my mind, I was feeling more positive about my outlook on life and myself as my awakening continued; but I still had a lot of programming to break through, so thinking something bad was going to happen instead of thinking something good might happen was perfectly natural for me, unfortunately. While all this craziness was going on in my head, I still had reality to deal with too, and it was about to get very real. I would say it's about to get strange, but this whole damn experience has been strange. Things were going a little better for me, and I was just trying to put as much distance as I could between me and that day I almost ended it all.

I didn't give a lot of thought about having to move west across the country because I thought it would probably never work out for me anyway. Part of me kind of thought maybe the guy interviewing me talked about it just to get me to take the job. It wouldn't be the first time in my life I was told less than the truth during a job interview.

People have told me things over the years, and I've gotten my hopes up just to have them crushed, so I wasn't about to let that happen to me again. There was always something or someone who would throw a monkey wrench into the plans I had. Besides, during my conversation with the person who ended up hiring me, he mentioned that the company had been working on this for years; and to be honest, he didn't sound really confident it would happen, at least not anytime soon. I thought I'd work there for a couple of years and then move on like I'd always done. I'd never been at a job for more than three or four years up till this point in my life anyway. I figured by the time this company got their crap together, I'd be gone; at least that's what I thought anyway.

A few more months went by, and life went on. It was the same old, same old every day; but in my world, trust me, that's not such a bad thing. I'd gotten used to talking to my higher self every day and dealing with the downloads I'd get and working through them. It all had become so very routine for me now. Most people, if they knew what I dealing with from day to day, would've thought my life is anything but normal. In fact, they would've thought it was completely freaking insane! Truth be told, if this wasn't happening to me, I wouldn't believe it was even possible to have this happen to a person.

Then one day, when I was doing my daily physical meditation, a voice—or a very loud thought anyway—said I'd be leaving Georgia not long after my brother moved from Georgia. After hearing this, I broke down and cried. I felt so happy and relieved because the past several months I was convinced that my brother's leaving meant that he was going to die somehow, but I was also really pissed off at my higher self for not telling me sooner. If this would've been made known to me months ago, I wouldn't have been stressed out of my mind the past several months, losing sleep and worrying about my brother. I was still confused by all this because I had never experienced anything like this before. This wasn't the kind of thing that people like me are supposed to experience in their day-to-day lives. I didn't really know what to think, but at the end of the day, at least I knew my brother was moving and not dying, and that was a damn good thing to say the least. I finally hoped I could get a good night's sleep, and trust me, I needed one.

I couldn't help but wonder how all this would work out because I hadn't heard anything from my brother or anything about him moving out of state, and my company hadn't said anything about being ready and needing me to move out west and take one of the positions they'd have out there either. I'd been thinking and wondering about all this stuff for a few days, and then, *bam*, it happened. Once again, I knew by now I shouldn't be surprised by anything that happened during this experience, but I still couldn't believe it. I got a call from my boss, and I almost crapped my pants because he told me in so many words to get my house on the market as soon as possible because they wanted me out there by the year's end. My first thought was, No flipping way. Things just kept getting stranger and stranger, but I hadn't heard from my brother yet; and as it turned out, I wouldn't have to wait very long.

Literally two or three days later, the phone rings, and it's my brother. *He*'s just calling to chat about nothing special, just the kind of conversation I'd had a thousand times before with him. This time, though, for me this telephone call from my brother would be anything but normal or routine. I don't remember exactly what we were talking about at first, but we'd been chatting for a while when the conversation turned to him and this woman he had been seeing for a while who just happened to live in Oregon where we grew up.

As we chatted about things, out of the blue he says he's decided to move to Oregon to live with her, and she's going to show him the ropes on how to get into the business she's in. It was something along those lines. I think it was something to do with insurance, but that's not what's important about the call. He said he would most likely head back there in the fall. As he was telling me this, I was in shock! I couldn't believe what I was hearing. I remember thinking, *You've got to be kidding me!* He was still talking, but now I was only hearing sounds on the other end of the phone. By the time I'd zoned back in on the conversation, he was telling me that he had to go, and we'd talk later about it.

I remember it was a Saturday we talked. After I hung up the phone, I had nothing else to do. I really felt the need to just relax and just contemplate some things. My chores were done, and my daughter didn't have any softball games either, so I was able to go upstairs to my "don't mess with me now" room to quiet my mind and reflect on everything that had been happening to me so far that year.

It was just another one of those times during this whole experience that it felt like I wasn't in control of my life or what was happening, and when I say that, I don't mean that in a bad or a negative way at all. It's just a really surreal feeling to have. Just imagine you're driving a car, but your hands aren't on the wheel; yet it's going right on down the road. Up in my room I was thinking, *What did it all mean?* When I thought about everything, my mind just spun as it usually did at first.

I wanted, no, I needed to get some perspective on everything because it was a lot to take in. I was used to strange and bazaar thoughts going on in my mind, but things in my mind are manifesting in the real world now. That's a completely different thing to deal with. What I mean is, things that I thought about and wanted to happen were happening. More and more this awakening or journey I'm experiencing is externalizing itself, and it's not just affecting me in my mind but also out in the real world too. It's like this awakening I'm going through has taken on a life of its own. Am I not in control of my life anymore? It feels like so many of my thoughts aren't my thoughts anymore either, like someone or something else is calling the shots and lining everything up into place for me.

It's funny. The first thought I had about all the recent events that were happening to me at that time was that I know nothing's happening to me but for me. It's just that I tend to forget that sometimes because my old programming takes over and tells me that all this stuff is happening to me. I'm reminded all the time that it's a very hard thing to do to overcome a lifetime of negative programming.

After a little bit of quiet meditation, some thoughts came to me. Thoughts and habits that the old me had acquired through a lifetime of unwise decisions were no longer going to be a part of my existence. They would serve no further purpose in my life anymore. The illusion of what I thought I was is gone, and it isn't coming back. It's like layer after layer of my misconceptions of what I am was being ripped from my mind. I was not only being stripped of my old way of thinking that didn't work and hadn't worked for me my entire life but now I was being removed from a place that wasn't going to work for me anymore. I knew I needed to live somewhere with a different vibration to it.

I've never really understood why I knew from early on in my awakening that I needed to get out of Georgia, but I did, and now it seemed that it was going to happen. I just knew that my time here was coming to an end. I was being led to or taken to where I needed to be to continue and complete this awakening. Knowing this was great, but that wasn't enough I still had to experience it. Whatever was coming next, it sure as hell wasn't going to be happening in Georgia that much I knew.

As I mentioned before, my intuition had become so sensitive. If I got a feeling about something or someone, it was always right, and

I mean always! I've learned to trust it and rely on it. About this time in my life, my intuition was telling me that something big was still coming. I'm not sure how, but I knew it wasn't me and my family moving; it was something else. My higher self communicates to me through the intuitive side of my brain, not the logical side. That still sounds crazy when I'm thinking about it and even crazier when I'm writing about it, but that's how it works. I had no idea what it would be like to write about myself. It's such a surreal thing to do because I'm just pouring myself out onto paper and opening up and revealing myself, not knowing what might come of it.

I hadn't told my wife about any of this stuff that was happening to me. I had no idea how to explain any of this to her. I mean I never said a damn thing since the very beginning of my awakening. It wasn't easy, but I knew it was the best for everyone. I never mentioned anything about what I was experiencing or about any of the downloads or imprints I'd received and was still receiving. I never told my wife how I got them or how often they came to me. I never told her how they've changed me inside over the years. My wife was not the kind of person to understand any of that kind of stuff. She's a very practical person. She gets up in the morning and deals with the challenges of that day. There've been so many times I wished I was like that, but I'm the complete opposite. I'm like a kite that's flying in the sky with my head in the clouds. I've always been a dreamer, and she's always been the grounded one with her feet firmly planted, keeping me from flying too high.

Our marriage works even though we're complete opposites, but we're opposite sides of the same coin. That's the key to our relationship; somehow, we're connected. We're connected in a cosmic way, and the reason why still hasn't revealed itself to me yet. I've had a lot of conversations about my relationship with my higher self, and it always responds by asking me this one question, and that's "What does your heart tell you?"

I'm always left with the profound sense and feeling that my wife and I were meant to be together, that's what my heart always tells me but for how long I don't know. One day I'll understand why. I know we're clearly two completely different people with totally opposite views on life and opinions on how to live it, but in the end, we're still just two souls helping each other grow and deal with this reality we're experiencing. It blows me away that we still find a way to experience life on our own terms, and yet we do it together, and we've been doing it for almost thirty years now. It's simply amazing! I feel like I chose my wife before I incarnated here this time around, but maybe it was designed by a higher power that knew I'd need her strength to get through to where I am today.

I let my wife make the decision on what state we should relocate to. I guess I hoped, by doing that, it would relieve some of the guilt I felt for wanting to move. I wanted to leave so badly for so long, but I knew my wife and daughter didn't. Where we were living just didn't feel right to me for quite some time. I struggled with this guilt for a long time, and I still find myself thinking about it from time to time, more often than I'd like to admit.

It's confusing because I knew it was inevitable, me leaving the state, but I still had these lingering doubts about whether it was a good or bad thing for my family. I had to trust the process and the path I was being led down. I really had no other choice. I was moving them to a place where they didn't know a single soul, not one person. I was forcing them to start over and forge a new life again. That's no small matter, but we're a tight family, my daughter, my wife, and I. This time I wasn't the only one that was going to be tested, but as a family, I know we'll get through whatever is thrown our way.

At the time all this was happening, I just couldn't get any clarity on any of it. It's like I could feel the path I was on, and I could see it laid out beneath my feet, but I couldn't see anything when I looked ahead. I had no idea if it was going straight for a while or if there was a big curve coming up. I understand that I was only allowed to see my life as it was happening right now. From time to time I'd be shown in my dreams just little glimpses of what was to come or what might come to pass. I was okay with that because I know, in time, I'd see what is to be.

I was told by my boss at the time I could choose from three different areas in California or one in Oregon, Utah, Denver, Washington, or Arizona. I told my wife, "If I'm going to move you from a place you don't want to leave, the least I could do was give you the choice of where we're going." We talked about it for a few days, and in the end, my wife chose Phoenix, Arizona. It was a great choice, and I was pumped that was the state, but I wasn't surprised. I'd had a feeling all along it would be Phoenix, but of course, I never mentioned that to my wife. I think that was one of my better decisions I made. It would've really pissed my wife off if she thought I already knew where we were going to move to.

I just had that damn feeling I get about things, and again things worked out for me. My entire life I've had a strong intuition, but what's different now is I trust it; and because I trust it, I can rely on it. Sometimes it feels like I have a superpower, and it's just one of the many beautiful things to come from my awakening experience.

As I'm writing this book and looking back on things, it's like pieces of a puzzle were being put in place for me. My higher self was working its magic, doing what I was never able to do; and like I said before, I was learning, knowing, and understanding more and more about myself, and that's something I can never put a price on.

Now it was time to sell the house, pack our stuff, say our goodbyes, and take this experience—this awakening of mine—on the road. I told you earlier I never say never anymore because anything and everything is possible in life, and I'm living proof of that. Life's just a dream, so dream on!

CHAPTER 11

The Confrontation

"Reflections of the way life used to be." Those are a few of the lyrics from a song written long ago, but that's exactly what I was doing when I drove away from the only life I'd known for the last ten years. It was a life that had begun for me in 2006 when I moved my wife and daughter, who was just two at the time, from Oregon to Georgia. I grinded my way through life for ten long years to carve out some sense of belonging and to feel I was home when I came through the front door of the house I'd bought. That achievement might seem like a simple or even trivial thing to many people, but not to me, and now all that was in my rearview mirror as I drove away!

I finally settled down and quit worrying about my wife and daughter who were going to be flying out to Arizona five days after I left Georgia with our two cats and two dogs. Then I was able to drive and put some miles behind me. I was caught up in the whole experience. I had gone through a lot of craziness to get to this moment. I felt like a little child, or anybody, I guess, for that matter, that was starting a journey and didn't know what to expect along the way or have any idea on how it was going to end. It felt magical as I drove out of the state I'd lived in for the past ten years. I felt free for the first time in God knows how long. I can totally relate to how people must feel after they're released from prison after doing their time.

The air smelled a little sweeter, the sky looked a little bluer, and the sun shined a little brighter that morning as I headed down the highway. It's strange because, I mean, I knew in one sense how all this came together, but at the same time I didn't know how everything had worked out so well for me up till this point. It's a weird feeling to have the sensation like you're sitting in the backseat while something else is steering and guiding you on your way through your life.

By this time now, to say my intuition had become a very powerful guide in my life would be an understatement, but there's more than that at work here. It feels like other entities are playing some role in all that's happened for me in my awakening, and that's just how it felt. I know it sounds crazy, but hell, this whole damn thing sounds crazy. I'm kind a struggling to explain it. Maybe it's a spirit guide or a guardian angel or maybe even a relative that's already crossed over. I'm not sure, but I know it to be true because thinking about it gives me that rush I talked about earlier in my writing, and that rush always reaffirms that I'm on the right track in my thought process.

You see, just a few months earlier, before I left for Arizona, I started having a lot of thoughts about guardian angels and spirit guides and things of that nature. When I began having those thoughts, I knew that my higher self was introducing me to new concepts. It just plants a little seed of thought, or what I like to call a "thought seed" in my mind; and the more I think about it, the more that thought grows. The more it grows, the more I begin to accept and understand what's being revealed to me. I know what you're thinking right now. "Damn, he's come up with another new term," and you'd be right, but again I digress.

The first day of my journey across this beautiful country came to a close. That first day was full of all kinds of emotions rushing through my mind, but mostly of hope and relief because I had survived everything that was thrown at me the last ten years and lived to tell the tale. That evening I found a cheap little motel, got some food, ate, and went to bed. I was completely drained and exhausted, but damn. it had been a good day for me. It was one of the best days of my life, no doubt about it. As I laid in bed and drifted off to sleep, I realized I had just a little bit of a smile run across my face because for the first time in quite a while, I was truly proud of myself.

All the excitement I felt and the long hours of driving had worn me down, but I was up early the next morning. I hit the road, and as I drove, I was treated to a beautiful morning sunrise with a soft pallet of yellow and orange colors blending together as only the "divine presence" could create. I was glad I was able to enjoy that time I had that morning because later that day all hell would break loose. That beautiful morning sunrise, as it turned out, was going to be the calm before the storm, and so it was.

The attack that began later that day was a cleverly calculated one. It was masterminded and led by my greatest adversary, a true wolf in sheep's clothing—my ego! Now, I could feel my higher self's presence and something else's presence too, so I knew I wasn't alone, but I also intuitively knew that this fight was my fight, just me against my ego. I've come to know and understand that I'm a warrior soul, and I knew this impending battle would be my first test of my spiritual growth and strength. I knew the deck would be stacked against me, and this wouldn't be a fair fight from the beginning because my ego wouldn't come alone, and I was right. My ego brought all six of its most persuasive and powerful minions with it. Those minions were the logical side of my brain and my five senses, and failure for my ego was not an option!

The attack came on so fast and so furious it felt more like an assault. My ego thought it would have an advantage over me because I'd be out on the open road and far from anyone I loved. I would be alone and vulnerable to its precision attacks on my mind. I was a little concerned because it had occurred to me when I left that morning that this would be the first time since all this began that I would be alone, but the first day couldn't have gone any better than it had, so I guess I thought I was in the clear, but

I couldn't have been more wrong. My ego is a brutally cunning opponent and was hoping I'd be feeling scared and alone, and then it would attack without restraint or any mercy, and so it did.

From nowhere, it began like a silent storm that came from deep within me, with nothing but negative thoughts pummeling my mind, questioning everything I had done and everything I had experienced since this whole awakening began just about five short years ago. My ego and its minions, which I just told you included the logical side of my brain and my five senses, attacked with a viciousness that was unparalleled in my life up till that point!

All of them had reigned over me and dominated me from my lower mind my entire life, but that was changing, and that was not acceptable to my ego. The first wave of negative thoughts that were conjured up were brutal and struck right at my heart. I was rocked and caught off guard because of two things, the verbal brutality of the attack and because the first day of my trip and the following morning had been so awesome! To be honest, I just never saw this attack coming.

My ego started in on me. "What were you thinking moving your family out of the state? What are you doing, leaving what took you ten long years, a decade, to build? Why are you screwing up your wife and daughter's lives? What made you think any of this crap would work? What are you going to do when this whole thing goes down the toilet? What makes you think moving across the country again is going to work now when it sure as hell didn't work the last time you did this? It seems failure is your goddamn middle name!"

I was starting to sweat and my heart felt like it was going to burst out of my chest. I was getting nervous and feeling short of breath. As I drove the truck, it was getting harder to concentrate and to pay attention to the road ahead of me. Before I knew it, the pure joy and contentment I felt just a short time earlier that morning was gone. I began to panic and began worrying. Is my ego's attack working? No, I have to fight it! I can't' let it beat me down! I can't give in to its control, but I was beginning to question myself, and doubt was setting in so quickly. My ego and its minions are so strong and persuasive, but I can't be this weak! Can I? This can't be happening. I've come so far in my journey, and I've learned so much. I just know my higher self has always been with me, and it's taught me and brought me so far. I have to fight with all my strength and all that I am. I know I can do this. I'll never let my ego and its minions control me ever again, and I mean never again!

Now my ego cranked it up a notch and got real nasty and began to rant and rave! My ego had heard enough. It couldn't listen to any more of what I was thinking, and it lashed out at me with a vengeance! It started in on me again.

"For God's sake, shut the hell up and quit your whining! Let me tell you something. You can't do anything without me! You don't have a goddamn clue what you're doing! You've never been strong enough to do what you're doing now! You weren't strong enough ten years ago when you tried this stunt moving across the country, and you sure as hell aren't strong enough now! Nothing's changed. You're still you, and you're still weak! You've always been weak. That's why I'm here! Just look at you now. You're out here in the middle of nowhere, and you're arguing with yourself! You're over the edge, and you've completely lost your damn mind, and you're not even smart enough to realize it! So much for guidance from your higher self! You're just so damn pathetic. You're just a joke. All you had to do was ask me what to do, and I'd had told exactly what to do, and it wouldn't have been this crazy crap you're pulling now, but I guess your new imaginary friend, your 'higher self,' had it all figured out for you, right? Everything except for the part about what you're going to do when you fall right on your ass out there in Arizona!

"What's your backup plan? Oh, wait. that's right. You don't have one, do you! Let me ask you something, genius. Where the hell was that prick your 'higher self' hiding the first forty-four years of your life? Where was it at when you were struggling and hurting all those years? Where was your higher self when you were lost and had no one to turn to? Who gave you strength and was there for you! You're goddamn right, I was the one there for you! Just me and my minions, as you call them, and no one else! You know I'm right, and you should listen to the logical side of your brain because it's part of the reason you're even here right now! Everything you've been doing the last five years is a result of that complete breakdown you had! It's okay, though, that's why I'm here. To help you! You see, when you think about it logically, you've never smelled, tasted, touched, felt, or even heard your so-called higher self at all, have you? That voice you say you hear in your head isn't real because you've lost your mind. Your batshit crazy, my friend! You're so broken up you had to invite this 'higher self' to help you cope with reality! If you think about it logically, you know I'm right, don't you?

"There never was another voice in your head except for mine. Me and the logical side of your brain and your five senses have been with you your whole worthless life, and we've never heard as much as a peep from your so-called higher self, and we sure as hell never experienced your so-called higher self either. Have I told you you're crazy? Because you are! You need me and my minions because we're all you have. Me and my minions got you through forty-four years of life, and let me tell you, there wasn't anything easy about it! You were always screwing everything up, and now you think you're just going to push me and my minions aside! That's not happening. You think you don't need me anymore? Yes, you do, so I'm not going anywhere! You've got another thing coming, my old friend. If you would've just listened to the logical side of your brain and paid attention to what your five senses were telling you and just done what you were told, then you wouldn't be in this horrible mess you find your-self in!

"All you ever did was screw stuff up! That's the only thing you've ever been really good at besides finding jobs, of course! I was the one who was always there with a plan, wasn't I? It was me and my minions that always kept you from losing touch with reality! I was always the one able to help you get medicated to ease your pain and the guilt you were feeling for being such a loser! I was the one that got you through one miserable day after another! Wake up for Christ's sake! Just wake up! It's only a matter of time before your family realizes you're batshit crazy. How much longer do you think you can hide it from them? Just let me get you back on track. All you have to do is what I tell you to do. You can do that, right? Be a good little boy and do what you're told."

Now it was my turn because I'd heard enough! I wasn't going to listen to any more of my ego's negative and condescending crap. My ego was so full of itself, but that was no surprise because that's its nature. I couldn't take any more. I was seeing things from a completely different point of view. Hell, I was seeing everything from a completely different point of view now. With the new understanding of myself, I didn't need my ego or its minions anymore. I know now they were the problem all along. My ego and its minions lied to me, manipulated me, and used me my entire life, and maybe my ego was right, though. Maybe I was weak, but I'm not anymore. That person is gone, and I think that's scaring the crap out of my ego. I sensed it, and so I fired back.

"Shut up, just shut the hell up!" I yelled back. I know I was talking out loud, but I didn't care. It was just me in the truck, and I was pissed now. "I've woken up. That's why I see now I don't need you anymore! I don't trust you anymore, not you or your minions! You don't care about me! You've never really cared about anything except yourself! You just used me to satisfy your own sense of power. To just satisfy what you are, and that's ego! You've done nothing but lie and manipulate me because that's what you're all about. It's in your nature. That's what you do! You're all about control and domination! You drove me to the point where I thought I had to kill myself to solve all my problems! I've listened to you my whole life, telling me that there is nothing more to this reality than what you and the logical side of my brain and my five senses say there is! I know now that's total bullshit! It was you that kept my higher self suppressed and separated from me deep down in the far reaches of the intuitive side of my mind! It was you that told me not to trust my intuition because you knew that's how my higher self was trying to reach me, and it was you that convinced me that you and my five senses knew better! It was you that always put me down and stepped all over my confidence!

"You knew if I was confident, I wouldn't need to listen to you, and I might start listening to my intuition, and you couldn't have that! You didn't want me using the intuitive side of my brain because you can't control that side can you! I wouldn't be so willing to give you control or listen to you if I knew about my higher self. You always made me question myself. You put just enough seeds of doubt in my mind to keep control over me. Well, fuck you! I'm done with you!" I screamed.

A lifetime of frustration was just pouring out of me. I was so damn angry, and I realized that tears were streaming down my face, but those tears were tears brought on by all the rage and anger I was purging and letting go of. It felt really good, and it felt really empowering to say what I said and to finally fight back against my ego my true nemesis.

This battle was far from over, though, and my ego lashed out at me again.

"Jesus, for all that's holy, just shut the hell up," my ego said. "Let me tell you something. Your higher self filled your head full of all this stupid crap you believe to be true now! Just how stupid are you? Can't you see what's going on? You've invented all this! It's all in your head! That day you had your breakdown, something snapped inside. You've never really recovered from that day. I could always feel it. You've never been the same since! Everybody sees it, just not you! Crazy people don't know they're crazy. Why? Because they're crazy. You need me and my minions more than ever now! There is no higher self, as you call it! I keep telling you if you would've just listened to the logical side of your brain, you would've known your 'higher self' is all in your head and didn't exist! You've been doing this all on your own the last five years, and now you're in way over your head! None of this should've ever happened, but you had to go and completely screw everything up that day you were supposed to kill yourself.

"It would all be over now, and I did it all for you! I had it all planned out for you! I did everything for you, Ryan! It's what I've been doing your whole pathetic life! I knew you didn't have the strength to go on. I knew you were at the end of your rope mentally. All you had to do was pull the damn trigger, and that's it, but you couldn't even do that. You couldn't even get that right. It took me years of giving you those negative thoughts about killing yourself and manipulating you to get you to the point where I thought you might actually have the balls to do it, but I see now I was wrong! You're just so weak. I didn't know just how weak you truly were until that day."

There was a sudden pause in the action, and the battle came to a screeching halt. I could feel my heart was beating like crazy, but I hadn't even noticed it till my mind went quiet. I wasn't sure what the hell was going on, and the silence was deafening. It's crazy. All I wanted from the time this fight began was for my ego to shut up, but when it did, it made me incredibly nervous. I don't trust my ego anymore, and I sure as hell wouldn't put anything past it either! I know I surprised it with how I stood up to it and didn't let it bully me. I know it was caught off guard because for the first time ever, and I mean ever, my ego is being challenged. I figured my ego was just regrouping and getting ready for another attack. My ego had retreated back down to my lower mind, no doubt. Probably strategizing with its minions on how to attack next. There was too much on the line, and my ego wasn't giving up that easily. After all, it is ego, and losing isn't something any ego would take very lightly. That much I knew to be true.

I was right, and I didn't have to wait for very long. My ego went right for the jugular, saving its best attacks for what would be its last assault. My ego knew it had attacked all my mental issues already, so it started right in on my physical handicaps this time. It knew I was very self-conscious about them, and so it thought a strategic attack on them would break me. My ego was going to use its minions to prove it's point that I not only wasn't all there mentally but that I also wasn't physically up to the task of calling my own shots and running my own life.

The first negative thought I heard it say in my mind was about my dyslexia. I'm severely dyslexic, and my ego knew it. Even though that happens in my mind, dyslexia manifests itself physically by writing things backward, flipping letters and numbers around and things like that. My ego reminded me with words not so kind that my wife pays all the bills because of that handicap I suffer from.

My ego was trying a different approach now and in a very calm manner basically said, "Look, Ryan, I don't know everything your 'higher self' has convinced you, or should I say more likely manipulated you into believing, but I hear from the logical side of your mind that you're wanting to write a book. Come on, that's the dumbest idea I think I've heard in a long time from you, and that's really saying something! You're just setting yourself up for some major disappointment. Just how are you going to accomplish that? Have you forgotten how dyslexic you are? You hardly read anymore because of it, and you flip your numbers and words all the time too. At least the ones you're even able to see anyway.

"I also know your wanting to speak to groups of people about your so-called awakening. Must I remind you that you're prone to stuttering when you get excited or nervous? And to be totally honest, you're just not smart enough to engage a large, or even a small group of people for that matter, and besides, no one wants to hear anything you have to say, trust me! Please, you have to let me take control. You're in no condition to do what you think you want to do. Look, my friend, I didn't want to say this, but you can't even lose weight, can you? How many years have you been trying and failing, miserably, I might add? Just look at yourself. You can see it's the truth. Your five senses don't lie to you. That's just the 'craziness' inside you telling you that. That's what I mean you've lost it, my old friend.

"You're just dreaming! Your head is full of delusions put there from your new imaginary friend. You need to let me help you before this charade of yours comes crashing down on you. When it does, it's not only you who will suffer but your family too! You know I'm right. I didn't want to go here, but I've seen the way your wife looks at you as of late, and it's so obvious she's losing faith in you. You know it's true. You can't just keep lying to yourself, but it's not too late to let me help you. All you have to do is submit to me and my minions and do what I tell you. If for no other reason, do it for your family before it's too late!"

My ego went on and continued in its much-calmer approach to the situation now. It was trying to throw me off guard or make me feel guilty for abandoning it, but I could feel the desperation in its tone and words that it spoke in my mind.

It said, "Hey, in that day, in that moment of weakness, you and the intuitive side of your mind invented your 'higher self,' but you see that's the problem with that side of your mind. It allows you to think freely. You're right, my friend. I have no control over the intuitive side of your mind, and that's why I hid it from you all your life. All it does is distort and confuse and complicate your sense of reality. People can't be allowed to just think for themselves without any guidance. Without me! Without their ego!"

It was the evening of the third day on the road, and there was another few moments of uncomfortable silence in my mind. Then I spoke, and when I did, it was out loud. I wanted to, no, I needed to hear myself say what I was about to say to my ego, and so I began, but I was too drained to yell or scream anymore.

I told my Ego that I loved it, and it will always be a part of me, but the days of it controlling me are over.

"I know I'm not what I'm going to be yet, but I also know I'm not the person you used to control anymore either. When you and your minions controlled me, I was lost, confused, and ignorant about everything. I didn't understand what I really was or why I was really here either, but that's all changed. My higher self has and is guiding and helping me grow from within. I don't receive and process information through my lower mind anymore. That's yours and your minions' domain, and I just have no more use of it. I'm trying to tell you as nice as I can. I didn't want it to come to this! Why can't you just be happy for me?"

My ego wasn't calm anymore, and it yelled back at me, "You ungrateful little man. After I've done for you! You think you can just toss me aside like some cheap little emotion or thought you're done with! I don't think so! You have no idea who or what you're screwing with, do you? I am your ego! You will serve me, and if you do, you just might make it till it truly is your turn to cross over! You obviously won't listen to logic anymore, and you clearly don't trust your five senses either, but humor me if you will and tell me, when did you finally find out that your five senses lie to you?"

I answered, "I've always felt they did, but that wasn't enough. I needed to truly know it, and now I do."

My ego answered and said, "Never mind, it makes no difference when or what you found out about me or my minions. It changes nothing. Do you hear me? It changes nothing!"

My ego spoke again, but I could feel it was frustrated and on the defensive this time.

"This isn't over. You think it is, but it's not over by a long shot. You may have won this little battle, but the war has just begun. I'm the true strength within you, not your higher self. I'll be right here. You said it yourself, I'm a part of you.

You can run, but you can't hide from me. Every chance I get, I'll be reminding you just how weak you are. Over time I'll wear you down until there's no choice but to summit and give me control and do what I say. Eventually, you'll see you're nothing without me."

When my ego finished, I fired right back, "I may hear from you in the future, that's true, but you will never control me ever again! You can count on that." I spoke out loud one last time and said, "I banish you, my ego and your minions, to my lower mind for the rest of my days. I need you no more, and I will no longer take council in what you say." And then I shouted, "Be gone, I will hear you no more!"

There was silence, and all I could hear was myself breathing. Slowly I tuned back in to what I was doing, and that was driving the truck. I don't know how I went through this experience the last couple of days without crashing. I know my ego's right; this won't be the last time I hear from it, but until then, at least I know I am getting stronger, and I'm not just imagining everything. I passed this test, but I'm sure there will be others along the way on this journey.

This battle with my ego was finally over, and it had raged on for two long days. The second and third days of my cross-country trip came and went. They were consumed with nothing but mind-numbing conflict and assaults from my ego. I don't remember what I ate those two days or where I stopped for fuel, and I don't recall where I stayed those nights either. What I do remember, though, is how incredibly drained I was after those two days of battling my ego. It's amazing how the body mimics the mind because my body felt like it been hit by a Mack truck too.

I slept like a man who had been pushed to his limits that third night and woke the morning of the fourth day of my trip feeling surprisingly very rested, clear-minded, and ready for anything that might come my way. I remember thinking, if I do ever write a book, the chapter about this experience will definitely blow people's minds because it definitely blew mine! I climbed behind the wheel of the rental truck that morning, and I couldn't help but reflect back on the previous two days as I rolled on down the road. I turned on the radio, and the first song I heard playing was one of my favorites, and so appropriate too. The song was "Highway Star" by the band, Deep Purple. I took it as a very good sign, and as I put my shades on, I felt another big smile come across my face as I began to sing along.

CHAPTER 12

The End...I Don't Think So

How the hell did I get from where I was all those years ago to here? That's a damn good question! It's the one question that I ask myself all the time! I think very few of us ever take the time to really reflect on our life journey. Sure, we talk about the good old days with friends at certain events or with family at family get-togethers, but when we're doing that, we're just talking about physical events that have taken place in the past. That's not what I'm talking about. I'm talking about the metaphysical aspect of our life journey.

Physical events in our lives are tied directly to the lower mind, which gets its information and tries to make sense of everything with the logical side of the brain and the five senses. The metaphysical events in our lives, however, are unseen events that happen within you. They happen within your mind. They're tied directly to the higher mind, which gets its information from the collective consciousness, which is beyond thought, and the higher mind makes sense of everything with the intuitive side of the brain.

Over the years, as my awakening experience continued, it was the abstract reasoning behind what I do in life and why I do it that I so desperately wanted to know and understand. I was drawn to wanting to understand it like a bee's drawn to honey. I would ask my higher self during my countless conversations with it, but I'd get no answer, or I'd get an answer I didn't like to hear. That happened far too often, but my higher self eventually always led me to the truth of the matter at hand.

So many times, simply asking the question of why I do what I do in life in conversations with my higher self brought on downloads and imprints with even more questions that I'd have to sift through and meditate on. Looking back, this is how it had to be for me because, for whatever reason, the long and hard way has always been my way. I'm pretty sure it's not like that for everyone, but for me this is how my sense of "knowing" was formed. First, the foundation of understanding was laid down. Once that was done and I truly accepted what I came to understand, I would get a strong sense of knowing that would permeate through me. It's hard to explain the feeling, but I liked it! It gave me a rush of energy.

I knew I was being given simple concepts to learn and understand at first, and when I learned them, I'd be given ones that were a little more advanced and so on. This would go on for as long as needed. It's like you can't just know and understand calculus mathematics when you first start learning your numbers. You have to start with simple mathematical concepts and gradually work your way up to where you get to the point where your mind can grasp much-harder concepts of numbers and what can be done with them.

When you have a profound sense of "knowing," it gives you a confidence that is unwavering and that's one of the rewards I cherish most from my awakening experience because I lacked and needed that attribute more than any other in my life. I began to see it was my sense of confidence given to me through knowledge I've gained during this whole experience, not my sense of belief, that was giving me the strength to endure over these past few years.

As time passed and I worked through my experience, I realized just how many of my actions and decisions were not my own. They were programs that were put there from the time I was born. They were put there by the television, neighbors, friends, family, religious leaders, teachers, politicians, and people I'd met along the way in my life's journey.

It was the illusion of thought that was taking place in my mind. I'd lived my entire life simply regurgitating what was put in my mind and thinking those were my thoughts. That's where my ego fits in. It made sure I kept on believing those were my own thoughts. It knew all along they weren't, but that's one of the ways how it controlled and dominated me all my life. It reinforced the programming. It lied and manipulated my thoughts, so I would do and act how it wanted me to. My ego only cared about the power and the control it wielded over me, and it could never have enough of either of them.

There's a quote by a person named Adyasha that I really love and appreciate at this point and time in my life now. It says, "Enlightenment is a destructive process. It has nothing to do with becoming better or being happier. Enlightenment is the crumbling away of untruth. It's seeing through the façade of pretense. It's the complete eradication of everything we imagined to be true." Everything I thought was truth was a lie, and I wanted and needed to discover what the truth was, and that's what my higher self was doing for me. It was emptying out my mind of all the programming and falsehoods that were put there during my life and then slowly filling it back up with knowledge so I could know, understand, and see the real truth of things. It took a lifetime to fill my head with all the crap that was in there, forty-four years to be exact, and it was going to take some time for my higher self to do its work. That's why my awakening has lasted as long as it has. The truth wasn't something I was able to accept right away. It took quite a while. The realization that all I knew was a lie wasn't something I could just accept overnight. In fact, at the very beginning of all this, I didn't even know the difference between truths or untruths.

I only knew what my ego and its minions had told me and showed me because I was a lower-mind thinker. Even as time went by, with all I've learned and with as much as I've grown spiritually and consciously, it was difficult to let go. The truth is a funny thing. On one hand, I've never been afraid of it, and it's something I've always chased after; but when I found it, most of the time it wasn't what I wished to hear and almost always not what I wanted it to be either. Truth is always a bittersweet pill to swallow, and knowing the truth always comes with a price. How big a price I have to pay depends on the seriousness or magnitude of the truth that I discover.

On my journey within, I had to learn to know things, not to just believe in things. I came to understand that belief was the roadblock to knowledge. For me it became a very obvious realization. Did I want to acquire the knowledge to know I could do whatever it is I wanted or needed to do, or did I just want to believe I could do it? We're taught from our religions from the time we're very young that all you need is faith. Nothing could be further from the truth than that. It wasn't faith that got me through the first five years of my journey or that terrible battle with my ego and its minions as I drove across the country. It was the knowledge I acquired over the years that gave me the confidence I needed to endure. To put it simply, I began to know I could do it, not just believe I could do it. I knew regardless of what I had to go through that I could get through it, period.

My whole life I believed in myself because that's what I was taught, but that left room for doubt to creep into my mind. It was a back door of sorts that my ego could use to plant those seeds of doubt that plagued me my entire life, but that's over now. The more I awaken spiritually and consciously during this journey of mine, the more I continue to acquire the knowledge of "self." It's that knowledge that has set me free and changed me and my life forever and put me on the path I'm on now.

This awakening I've been going through has been and still is the most incredible thing I've ever experienced, but my journey within has also been in many ways just as terrifying. As time passed, I came to understand it and embrace it. I don't know if it's because I've changed so much and saw things so differently or if I've just become more confident with the whole process, or maybe it's just because I understand what I am. I think it's most likely a little of everything.

It's sometimes hard for me to believe how this whole experience has changed me; yet at the same time, in some ways, I'm still the same old me. This may sound weird, but I'm me, and yet I'm not me. It's a really bazaar thing because I guess I never expected to feel this way. To be honest, I really didn't know how I'd feel. At the beginning, I remember thinking that whatever is happening to me or whatever I'm going through, when it's all over, if I make it to the end, I hope I'm better for it. I've been through a lot of shit in my life, and I've always come out on the losing end or the wrong end and haven't been better off for it, but not this time. This time I've been learning and growing in the most beautiful way with every day that passes. I understand what I truly am, and I've said it before, my friends, that's priceless!

Other people have made this wild journey within themselves and survived, but there are others out there that don't know what's happening to them, just as I didn't know what was happening to me. I know because I can feel them out there. They're confused, scared, depressed, and so very alone, but I'm out here with you, and I just want them to know they're not alone. That's why I put my thoughts down on paper and revealed all of myself to you in this book in hopes of connecting with those special people who might be experiencing what I experienced but don't know what it is yet. Those people are having a strange feeling right now that something is coming or about to happen, but they don't know what, and it's a feeling they've never felt before. I'm here to tell you that what you may be experiencing or about to experience is an awakening, which is truly an experience like nothing you've ever experienced! I can promise you that, but don't be afraid to become what your true self wants you to be. Remember you were chosen, which means you're a warrior soul, and that means you have the strength to endure an awakening. You just don't know it, but you will in time.

If your eyes don't just look but they see, if your ears don't just listen but they hear, and if your heart doesn't just beat but it yearns for understanding and knowledge, then these words I've written will resonate with you on some level. If, however, you read my words, and you come away thinking I'm just batshit crazy, that matters not because it just means it's not your time...yet!

I have many titles that I'm known by in this life. Some of them are father, husband, brother, son, friend, coworker, neighbor, to name a few, but the one I cherish the most of all is the one I call myself when I'm alone in the quiet of the night, "The awakened."

I know my journey isn't over yet. In fact, it has just begun!

ABOUT THE AUTHOR

As a self-taught writer with no previous writing experience, Ryan was able to finish this, his first book, in just under a year. He enjoys a lifelong passion of playing the drums, and he plans on writing many more books in the coming years.

Ryan D. Burd was born in Toledo, Ohio, 1966. He lived there until he was ten. His parents then moved to Beaverton, Oregon, where he grew up and lived until 2006. He and his wife and daughter then moved to Georgia.

In 2016 he relocated to Arizona where he presently lives.

CPSIA information can be obtained
at www.ICGtesting.com
Printed in the USA
LVHW092334081120
671116LV00005B/170